I0119558

Defining Obama

Leadership Perspectives of the First African-American President of the United States

Peter R. Garber

First Edition

Multi-Media 🔖))
P u b l i c a t i o n s   I n c.

Oshawa, Ontario

Defining Obama: Leadership Perspectives of the First African-American President of the United States

by Peter R. Garber

Managing Editor:	Kevin Aguanno
Copy Editor:	Susan Andres
Typesetting:	Peggy LeTrent
Cover Design:	Troy O'Brien
eBook Conversion:	Agustina Baid

Published by:
Multi-Media Publications Inc.
Box 58043, Rosslynn RPO
Oshawa, ON, Canada, L1J 8L6

http://www.mmpubs.com/

Paperback	ISBN-10: 1554890659	ISBN-13: 9781554890651
Adobe PDF ebook	ISBN-10: 1554890667	ISBN-13: 9781554890668

Published in Canada.

CIP data available from the publisher.

Table of Contents

Preface

Defining anyone as complex as Barack Obama is a daunting, if not impossible, task. President Obama is arguably a unique U.S. president in history. His heritage redefines diversity for American politicians. His abilities as a politician and leader often transcend description. He has become a uniquely appealing political icon in a short period. The world responded to his election as president of the United States with unprecedented enthusiasm, and as his presidency begins his legacy, he seems destined for great things to come.

Much of Obama's appeal is his ability to relate to so many different people from such a variety of backgrounds. Although, we might never be able to truly define Obama, learning to understand him better can help us better understand ourselves. Somehow, we each see part of ourselves in him, regardless of our politics, race, or position in life. He seems to reach that part of us that gives us hope for a better future and helps us better understand and define ourselves.

Barack Obama's life itself is truly an American story, proving once again that, in this great country, anyone has a chance to grow up and become president. Obama's achievement of becoming the first African-American president is not only an inspiration to blacks, but to all Americans. This book highlights Barack Obama's many different dimensions and includes definitions to help tell the story of how a young boy born in 1961 to parents of different racial backgrounds and growing up in such distant places as Hawaii and Indonesia could grow up to be president. These dimensions appear in gray boxes throughout this book, as they relate to the Barack Obama's life story and help to define him as the person he is now.

Every leader is a product of his or her past. They are the total of all their experiences and the people who influenced their lives growing up. These experiences shape the leader and influence his or her decisions and actions as they rise to a position of power. Barack Obama was able to use his diverse background and past to help him relate to potential voters during his successful presidential campaign. This diversity defined Barack Obama as a leader, helping him attract the legions of people who supported him on his journey to becoming the first black president of the United States of America. His is a fascinating story of a boy growing up in several different cultures and his search as a young man to find his own identity. This book explores Barack Obama's leadership characteristics and shows how these abilities can help you as a leader, if you are in a leadership role or in any role you play in life. You can learn much by better understanding what led Barack Obama to the most powerful leadership position in the world, so read on.

In Search of Leadership

The world is always in search of great leadership. We revere our leaders. Leaders often mark the beginning of a new era or the end. They offer hope and promise for the future and the change necessary for the dream to be realized. Often, a newly elected president tries to represent what his predecessor failed to deliver. Presidential candidates promise to change what is currently wrong with the country without their influence. All the 2008 presidential candidates promised to change what was wrong with the country at that time. The Bush administration had provided many campaign issues for all the presidential hopefuls to address, as they promised to make the country better in the future. In many ways, President Bush made it easy for all the major candidates to provide a better vision for the future. But how did Barack Obama rise above the others to win the presidency? The answer is his leadership. Obama was able to convince voters that he was the one who could lead the country in the right direction, despite the many obstacles and odds against him.

An Improbable Candidate

Barack Obama was an improbable candidate for president of the United States from the beginning. When he entered the presidential race in 2007, he did not fit the image of what was traditionally thought of as a presidential hopeful. He was inexperienced in politics, young, and unknown on the national scene until just a few years earlier. He had an unusual name easily confused with an infamous terrorist. He spent much of his youth outside the continental United States, and even outside the country, and he was entering his party's presidential primary race against a powerful political family with considerable momentum toward the White House. And one more thing—he was black. You certainly would not have guessed that this profile would lead to a successful run for the presidency of the United States of America.

But he did win. Barack Obama won the presidency by a significant margin on November 4, 2008, against a traditional opponent representing nearly everything that he was not. John

McCain was an American hero. His father was a Navy admiral; he was well known for being a prisoner of war in Viet Nam, enduring years of torture but never giving in to his captors' horrific abuse; and he had a distinguished career in the United States Senate for many decades. McCain symbolized the white establishment and American ideals, as he aggressively sought the office for many years with powerful friends supporting him. It seemed that his time had finally come.

However, it was not to be. Barack Obama presented America with a different choice, one promising something new. He promised change. Change, or, more accurately, the promise of it, is the most powerful political force on Earth. Obama harnessed this power to help propel him to the White House in ways that had not been seen in many decades, even generations. As one supporter described him, "I don't see Obama as a politician but rather as a leader," perhaps the highest praise any politician running for office can receive. He promised a better America, one in which anything is possible to achieve if you can dream big enough. He not only promised change; he was a living example of what could be achieved.

Adventurous

One thing Obama inherited from both his parents and maternal grandparents was a sense of adventure. His father left his native Kenya to pursue an education in such a far-off place as Hawaii, the newest state in the U.S. He was eventually drawn back to his home country, but it was not before marrying an American student he met at the University of Hawaii. She would give birth to a son who would one day become president of the United States. Obama's mother, Stanley Ann Durham, also was an adventurous soul, marrying two men during her lifetime from distant countries and living much of her adult life in her second's husband's native country of Indonesia. Even his grandparents seemed to have wanderlust, moving from Kansas to the state of Washington, and then to

Hawaii. This sense of adventure he apparently inherited led him from Hawaii to Los Angeles to New York City to Chicago and eventually to Washington embarking on an ambitious journey to become the first African-American president of the United States.

CHAPTER 1

Leadership
Perspectives

Leadership is a matter of perspective, constantly influenced by time, place, and circumstance. This perspective is as a kaleidoscope that changes with a leader's every new life experience. Leaders see the world through their own unique perspectives, shaped by virtually every experience they have had up to the point they become leaders. These experiences, which eventually define who they are and become, shape leaders. They, too, are the total of their experiences. The steps of the Leadership Perspective Model help shape and establish what all leaders will become and what they will be known for achieving during their time in leadership roles. Each step of the model influences the next, creating a basis or foundation that will last a lifetime.

```
┌─────────────────────────────────┐
│   5. Capitalizing on Success     │
└─────────────────────────────────┘
┌─────────────────────────────────────┐
│   4. Finding Formula for Success      │
└─────────────────────────────────────┘
┌──────────────────────────────────────────┐
│   3. First Attempts                         │
└──────────────────────────────────────────┘
┌──────────────────────────────────────────────┐
│   2. Character Builders                         │
└──────────────────────────────────────────────┘
┌──────────────────────────────────────────────────┐
│   1. Early Experiences                              │
└──────────────────────────────────────────────────┘
```

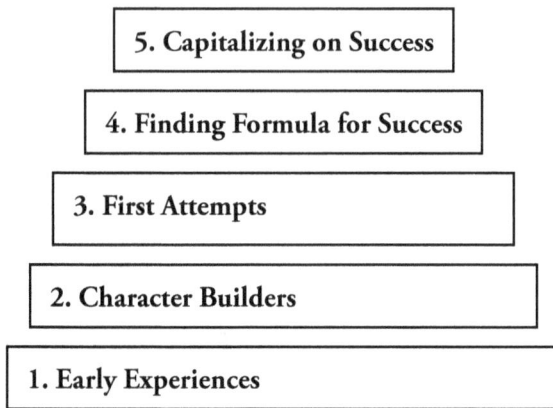

The Leadership Perspective Model

The Leadership Perspective Model shown above illustrates the major influencers shaping a leader's perspective and, ultimately, how he or she leads others. Each influencer in the model is sequential with each successive step, influencing the next. The five steps in the model are Early Experiences, Character Builders, First Attempts, Finding Formula for Success, and Capitalizing on Success.

Early Experiences

Each of us is a product of our family, upbringing, childhood experiences, and so forth. These elements all create who we are today. They also influence our potential and eventual ability to be effective leaders. Learning more about the early years of leaders such as Barack Obama is always interesting. By studying the lives of these men and women, we gain insights into what shaped their leadership perspectives later in life. Legendary leaders emerge from all lifestyles—some born into privilege, others into poverty. Perhaps most interesting is the diversity of the great leaders' early childhood experiences. Obviously, great people do not come from one background or economic status.

What is more important is what these leaders learned from their childhood experiences that eventually brought them to the powerful roles they would play later in life, enabling them to become great leaders.

Character Builders

Character is a concept hard to define but easier to recognize. We might describe a leader as having great character, but never specifically understand what "great character" means. Character is a complicated concept. To say that someone has great character is saying that he or she has high integrity, morality, spirit, personality, quality, and so on. The question of whether character is learned or inherited might be debatable, but it should suffice to say that early childhood experiences greatly influence a leader's character. Character builders also come from any variety of experiences. Many might believe in the "school of hard knocks" theory of character building. The harder one's early childhood experiences, the more character is built. But character building is not exclusive to difficult or hard childhood experiences. Character is built from potentially all our early experiences. Most important is what we take from these early experiences and how we use what we learn later in life.

First Attempts

Wouldn't it be great if the first time that you attempted something, you were successful? Unfortunately, this is seldom the case. Success usually involves many previous failed attempts. Again, what is most important is what we learn from our failures that can help us become successful later in life, particularly in a leadership role. The lives of great leaders are filled with failures, just as in our lives. They, too, have had disappointments and times in their lives when they might have felt that they would never be successful. There is often a fine distinction between success and failure. A commonality of most great leaders is that they did not give up easily or quickly. They consider failure as a learning opportunity. For them, failure only means that something different needs to be done next time.

Finding the Formula for Success

Success does not come in a bottle nor is there somewhere you can go to find an exact formula for success, which might not be an exact scientific formula like one found in a chemistry laboratory, but one that works for you. You must find your own formula for success. We all have a formula for our own success. We learn what works and does not work for us. The same is true for great leaders. They found something enabling them to be successful. Again, this formula might have been discovered after many failed attempts trying different things. This formula might have been discovered early at anytime later in life. The most important thing is that this formula is recognized. So often, people find this formula for their success and do not recognize its value. They continue searching for their key to success, even after discovering this formula.

Capitalizing on Success

At the top of this model is capitalizing on one's success. The key for most great leaders is that once they discover this formula for success, they recognize its worth and allow it to continue to work for them. They refine and develop the key to their success and usually do not deviate far from it, which, at times, might not always be a wise or good thing to do, depending on the circumstance. If you are unable to adapt to changing times and circumstances, your past successes might become your greatest liabilities if you cannot change. The greatest leaders understand this and know that capitalizing on success does not necessarily always mean doing the same thing. Great leaders recognize the time to change, regardless of how successful something might have been in the past, or otherwise, they will fail.

This book explores each step of this Leadership Model to examine in more detail how President Barack Obama's life fits into it. What will be presented are many of the lesser-known facts about Obama's life leading to his rise to the presidency and their influence in shaping who he is as a leader now.

CHAPTER 2

Early Experiences

Blessed

Barack Obama was named after his father, Barack Hussein Obama Sr. Barack means "blessed" in Arabic. He was obviously blessed with extraordinary natural abilities and many people in his life who cared about him in his extended family, including his mother, grandparents, stepbrothers and stepsisters, and a beautiful wife and two adorable daughters.

Barry Obama. That is the name by which Barack Obama was known during his childhood days until the time he was in college, even though he was born Barack Hussein Obama II. Barry was the name his father, Barack Hussein Obama Sr., had adopted when he came from his native Kenya to Hawaii to study in 1960. The senior Obama perhaps felt, as many others moving to the United States for the first time, that it would be better to have an "Americanized" name to more easily fit in. Just think how different Obama's candidacy for president might have been had he kept his childhood name rather than reverting to his birth name and that of his father. The name Barry Obama might have been less controversial, easier to remember, and well, more American. Just think of campaign signs such as "Vote for Barry Obama for President." Do you think anyone would have given his name much thought? Perhaps not. There must have been times when his campaign staff had wished that he had stuck with his boyhood name. But that he did return to his birth name tells us much about Barack Obama. It speaks of how he searched for his identity as a young man after growing up in several different environments as an African-American youngster. It might also be evidence that Obama never seriously envisioned running for public office, as he made this conscious decision to adopt such a different name when he had the choice to remain known as Barry rather than Barack. On the other hand, perhaps his success was because of his embracing his identity and heritage—who knows?

His mother, Stanley Ann Durham (her father wanted a son, hence her first name), was raised in several places, including the state of Washington, Texas, and eventually, Hawaii. She was only 18 when she gave birth to Obama and spent only about 12 years living with her son, as her interest and career as an anthropologist continuously drew her to distant Indonesia where she raised her son until he was 10 years old. Despite her absences, she had a strong and significant influence on young Obama, providing love, guidance, and perhaps her sense of adventure and willingness to follow her heart. "When I think of my mother," Obama told a reporter, "I think there was a combination of being grounded in who she was, what she believed in. But also a certain recklessness. I think she was searching for something. She wasn't comfortable seeing her life confined to a certain box."

Obama lived in Jakarta, Indonesia, for about five years with his mother and her second husband, Lolo Soetoro, a military leader who was called back to his country after attending college in Hawaii where he met Obama's mother.

There, Obama had early childhood experiences such as having crocodiles living in his backyard, and he recalls a man with leprosy coming to the door of their home one day, begging for money. As much as young Obama was intrigued with this faraway exotic place, his mother worried that her bright young son was not being intellectually challenged. Despite her efforts to supplement her son's education at the time with early morning tutoring sessions, she was disappointed in the quality of education he was receiving and sent him back to Hawaii to live with her parents in 1971 when he was in the fifth grade through his graduation from high school. There, he attended the Punahou School, an exclusive private school he was able to attend because of his scholastic achievement and some financial aid. His mother returned to Hawaii in 1972 for five years, and then in 1977, went back to Indonesia, where she continued to work as an anthropologist. She stayed there until returning to Hawaii in 1994. She died of ovarian cancer in 1995.

Obama recalls what it was like being the new kid at the Punahou School with such a different background and appearance from just about everyone else, especially when the other kids learned of his father's African heritage and his real name. "A redheaded girl asked to touch my hair and seemed hurt when I refused. A ruddy-faced boy asked me if my father ate people." Obama once even told his classmates the story that his father was a Kenyan prince.

His father was a mystery to him, distant and missing for virtually all of his namesake's life. Most of his knowledge about his father was in the form of family stories told and retold by his grandparents about their unique, but brief, experiences getting to know the senior Obama during the few years he was married to their daughter. He was highly intelligent, well spoken, and charismatic—qualities he would pass on to his son. Barack Obama only spent a month with his father, shortly after returning to Hawaii from Indonesia when he was 10, but spent much of his life as a young adult trying to learn more about him and, consequently, about himself. The brief month he spent with his father was highlighted by a visit by Obama Sr. to Barry's fifth grade class to talk about his native country and its struggle to be free. The students seemed to get the message that every person is struggling in some way to be free. The visit also included a family quarrel that ensued about Barry being able to stay up to watch a Christmas favorite special, *How the Grinch Stole Christmas*, with his father insisting that he go to his room and study instead and leaving young Barry looking forward to the end of his father's visit.

Barack Obama chronicled much of this journey of identity in his first book, *Dreams of My Father*. The then young Barry knew his grandparents, Madelyn and Stan Durham, as Toot (grandmother in Hawaiian) and Gramps. His grandmother worked her way through the ranks at a bank to vice president, and his grandfather, a furniture salesman, later sold insurance in Hawaii.

Diverse

Obama is unquestionably the most diverse president in history, but his diversity goes beyond his multiracial and cultural heritage. Even though he was born in Hawaii, and he spent much of his early youth in Indonesia before returning to Hawaii, Obama made a conscious effort, beginning as a young man, to expand his horizons even beyond the diversity in which he was raised as a child. He seemed to realize that he had much to learn about himself and the black community. Instead of seeking more lucrative and prestigious positions after graduating from Columbia University and working as a writer in New York for several years, Obama sought the role of a community organizer—one not all that easy to find at the time. He seemed to be seeking a more diverse experience than his years in college living in Los Angeles and New York

City offered. He sought to find and live the black inner city experience that he had been somewhat sheltered from during his youth. Obama would later say that working on the South Side of Chicago as a community organizer was the best education that he could experience, and he relied heavily on these diverse experiences to promote and prepare him for future political offices.

Obama grew up as a multiracial child on the island of Oahu, Hawaii—a state admitted to the union only a few years before his birth. Hawaii, although much more of a multiracial melting pot than any other state or perhaps anywhere in the world, still had its share of prejudice and its own unique challenges and problems for the young Obama as a boy, although it would take a few years before he would even understand the concept of prejudice. Obama would later write in his first book, reflecting on what he saw in a family photo album, "That my father looked nothing like the people around me, that he was black as pitch and my mother was white as milk—barely registered in my mind." Hawaii consists of native Hawaiians, Japanese, Filipinos, Samoans, Okinawans, Chinese, and Portuguese, along with Anglos and a smaller population of blacks, traditionally centered in the military installations. Obama was still different from almost everyone else around him with a few blacks living on the islands. There is no doubt that these experiences significantly affected Obama and helped shaped the man he would become. It was not just a matter of being black but not understanding what being black really meant. Obama sought out blacks throughout his youth, but it was not the same as growing up as a young black kid on the mainland. Barry Obama was raised by non-blacks, spending most of his youth living with his white maternal grandparents in Hawaii, except for the years he lived in Indonesia with his mother and her Indonesian second husband.

These experiences helped give Obama a unique ability to understand and relate to others different from him. Saying that you understand people different from you is one thing; living in these different cultures is something entirely different. Just think of what it would be like to hear the dinner conversation every night of people born into a different race than you were. On the presidential campaign trail many years later, he would say that he could relate to many of the white middle-class voters he met because they reminded him so much of his white grandparents who had originally come from Kansas. Their values were imprinted on Obama as a young boy as he grew up in their home. How many black candidates for political office can make such a claim?

Engaging

Throughout his life, Obama has always had an engaging personality. He is interested in other people and listens to what they have to say. Later in his life, he became a community organizer to be more engaged in the black community, especially in an inner city urban area such as the South Side of Chicago. These experiences helped create a balance between his Ivy League education and the less advantaged in our society. Obama learned to live in both worlds, taking valuable life lessons from both experiences. Perhaps his ability to engage with such a wide variety of people is his greatest strength as a politician and public servant.

Defining Moments

Just think about how these early years shaped Obama's unique and extraordinary life. How do you think these experiences helped him rise to the presidency of the United States? Do you think that he could have become who he is now without having had these experiences?

There is no doubt we are who we are now as the total of our experiences, both good and bad. Sometimes, the most difficult experiences have the strongest and most beneficial influence on our lives. Think about how your own early experiences help shape and develop who you are now. If you are a leader, think about how the experiences help you better understand and relate to the people you influence. The next chapters of this book explore how life's experiences help develop character.

CHAPTER 3

Character Builders

B arack, or Barry at the time, is remembered by his
classmates at the Punahou School as an unassuming kid,
good-natured, and always smiling. He was well liked
and known to have a good sense of humor. He was also a good
student, who could easily complete assignments with little
effort, compared to many of his classmates who had to work
much longer and harder to achieve similar academic results.
He could write a school report in one sitting at the typewriter,
instead of laboring for days or weeks on the same project, as
did many of his friends. He liked books and jazz but loved
basketball. He was consumed by his interest in basketball,
constantly dribbling a ball; idolizing black NBA stars of the
time such as Dr. "J", Julius Erving with his amazing moves;
and practicing his jump shot every opportunity he got. His
early aspiration was to become a professional basketball player,
showing little interest in politics as a youngster growing up in
Hawaii.

He was more globally focused than the rest of his
classmates—understandable considering his early experiences
in life. He could talk intelligently about world events, such as
issues in the Middle East and problems around the world, and

took much more of an interest in these current events than his peers took. These early experiences perhaps helped shape Obama's political skills years later, as he would become known for his ability to see the bigger picture, to understand and relate to the situation of others, to care about others, and to be willing to do something to help their lives. He was also known to be social, and he related to many different groups of friends. He is remembered as a good communicator, even as a youth. He was not afraid to speak up and often said what everyone else might have been thinking but was reluctant to say. He had a comfortableness, and even pizzazz, attracting others to him.

However, none of his friends and acquaintances seemed to be aware at the time of the inner struggle that Barry Obama was experiencing. His search for himself was not evident. He seemed content with his interest in basketball, jazz, books, and hanging around with friends, including other African Americans. Not until he wrote his memoir, *Dreams of My Father*, did even the people closest to him at the time know these strong inner feelings.

Obama is candid about these feelings in his autobiographical book, admitting to drinking and using drugs, including marijuana and cocaine. Despite his academic abilities and potential, he did not apply himself in high school, instead concentrating more on his beloved basketball. Later, he said that admitting to using drugs during that period of his life perhaps was not a politically astute thing to write about, but he did not shy away from the disclosure, as did another baby-boomer president, Bill Clinton. In contrast to Clinton's famous, "I didn't inhale" excuse for smoking marijuana, Obama admitted that, when he was a kid, he inhaled, saying that was the whole point of smoking marijuana in the first place. The public certainly was not used to hearing this candor from presidential candidates about themselves, and it might have been why his smoking marijuana never became a major political issue for him.

Obama began his college education at Occidental College, a small liberal arts school in Los Angeles and transferred to Columbia University after his sophomore year. At Occidental, he began to change his views about the world and himself. Although still not taking school as seriously as he should, he became more aware of his black heritage and began going by his birth name, Barrack.

Obama reflects on his years at Columbia University as the pivotal time in his life when he stopped getting high and focused on his studies and what he wanted to do with his life. In his memoir, he describes himself in terms that are more solitary—learning about what it was like being black in New York City, even bathing in an open fire hydrant the first morning he found himself in the Big Apple. He majored in political science and international affairs at Columbia, perhaps influenced by his early years living with his mother in Indonesia.

After graduating from Columbia, Obama pursued his interest in becoming a writer, working as a junior editor for a small newsletter and publishing firm helping companies with international operations understand foreign markets. His supervisor there believed that he would someday become a novelist. Obama took charge of updating *Financing Foreign Operations*, a yearbook editing manuscripts from correspondents in 40 countries. Obama also wrote for *Business International Money Report*, a newsletter that covered currency issues and monetary policy. The people with whom he worked remember him as somewhat aloof and seldom socializing with coworkers. He occasionally engaged in debates with coworkers about such issues as trade and apartheid in South Africa.

After about a year at Business International, Obama found a job as a community organizer in Chicago, a decision that would be considered an unlikely career move for most. However, Obama had a different vision for his future and himself. Obama, for reasons perhaps only he understood, had set his sights at that time in his life on becoming a community organizer. Perhaps he felt that he needed to do something for others less fortunate, or he needed to understand his own identity as a young black man better. Whatever his reasons, Obama made it clear, as he left his colleagues and friends in New York City and set off for the South Side of Chicago to become a community organizer, that he had more important things to do with his life.

Focused

It would have been easy for Obama to forget about the needs of the underprivileged in Chicago with his Ivy League undergraduate degree and personal attributes that could have opened more lucrative-paying and more glamorous career opportunities for him at the time. However, he focused on making a difference for the people needing help and continuing on his own personal journey of self-awareness and discovery. This focus on community service has continued throughout his political career.

However, finding this opportunity in the first place was not easy, as Obama had to send his résumé out to many potential employers to become a community organizer. He was eventually hired by a New Yorker living in Chicago named Gerald Kellman. Kellman hoped to organize Chicago's South Side churches whose congregations were suffering from the economic decline of the steel industry. The problem he was encountering was that, being white and Jewish, the black church membership and clergy could not relate to him. He needed an African American these people could embrace and someone who could unite these churches and communities.

From Obama's resume, Kellman was unsure whom he would meet with the name Obama (he thought he might be Hawaiian) when he arranged for an interview with him at a coffee shop on New York's Upper West Side. Kellman needed to be comfortable with why someone with Obama's credentials and potential would want such an unglamorous job. Obama said that he wanted to make a difference, to help change things for the better, and that he was seeking a "grass roots" opportunity and wanted to learn. Keller hired him on the spot, offering him a $10,000 salary and $2,000 to buy an old Honda to get himself moved to Chicago.

A month later at age 23, Obama was on the job conducting 20–30 interviews with members of the churches and community. It was 1985, just two years after Harold Washington, Chicago's first black major, was elected, and he had energized the black community of Chicago with hope for the future. Community organizers are not supposed to set the agenda for the people they are trying to help. Their goal is to inspire and motivate community members to make changes that can make a real difference in their lives. Obama tried to assure the people he met when he first arrived on the community scene in Chicago that he was there to learn with them about how to make positive change happen. There, he began his education in the political system, as he tried to help the disadvantaged and underprivileged get just some of their basic needs and rights in life.

Obama later said that this experience helped him learn to listen to people, rather than come in with a predetermined agenda to impose on others. Even at this young age and inexperience, Obama impressed the people with whom he worked in those early Chicago days with his poise, comfortableness with himself, authority, and presence. These qualities gave confidence to the people he tried to help that they, too, should have the same self-respect and hope for the future, even though he looked so young and innocent at the time that some candidly referred to him as "Baby Face." The three years he spent working as a Chicago community organizer taught him many lessons about people and about himself. He learned that it was not about him, but the people he tried to help needed to be the focus and to be most important. He learned that you must work through and with the system, not against it.

He also got his first taste of the hardball realities of politics but, in this case, more about inner city turf wars and local power struggles. These local issues might seem trivial, compared to more worldly issues he would later face as president, but they were still important to the people directly affected at the time. He learned how to mobilize people to act toward a common goal, rather than individual self-interests, even when dealing with politicians or clergymen, for that matter. He learned that being too idealistic can be a problem, especially if you lose credibility as a result. He adapted objectives that were more pragmatic and found ways to build interest from a grass roots beginning. He was not afraid to try to do something difficult and worked tirelessly to achieve goals. Working out of a small church office, Obama knocked on doors, trying to make 25 new contacts per week in neighborhoods on the South Side of Chicago—an effort that well would have discouraged someone else with less ambition and desire to positively change this community. He helped the citizens of Chicago's disadvantaged neighborhoods learn how to make this change happen for them. He taught them that making their point in a respectful manner, rather than with anger would yield much better results. Anger, he taught them, just takes away your focus from what you are trying to accomplish, and being civil during confrontations with authorities is how to obtain what you are seeking from public officials. He also taught them not to just point out problems, but also to recommend practical solutions to these problems that the funding they sought would achieve.

He was known, even in those days, as a meticulous planner, rehearsing with the citizens everything they were to say to public officials and how to make the best impression. Obama earned the reputation of being able to get public funding that many others were seeking, using this approach. One such project was to pursue authorities to remove asbestos from a decrepit public housing project named Altgeld Gardens. No garden spot, the two-story row houses had been built for black World War II veterans and were ringed with toxic waste sites. Obama also worked to try to unite blacks, Latinos, and whites from turning on one another, as they lost their jobs during those difficult times in Chicago, and to promote job training programs in these neighborhoods. He took copious notes during those community organizing days, often holing up in his Hyde Park apartment, writing short stories about the people with whom he worked. These stories would someday be included in his future best-selling book, *Dreams of My Father*.

In 1982, Obama received the news that his father had been killed in an automobile accident in Kenya. It was not until years later, when he was living in Chicago, that he would meet his older half-sister and learn a more accurate account of his absent father. The elder Obama, after graduating from Harvard, returned to Kenya to work for an American oil company and then for the country's Ministry of Tourism. Eventually, he fell out of favor with the people in power and became a heavy drinker, an abusive husband, and a social outcast. This account was different from what he had understood from the stories he heard growing up about his father. Perhaps those stories were an attempt to fill in the void his father's absence created over the years with a more positive image that he could be proud of and emulate. The truth in some ways set Obama free to become the man he wanted to become, rather than chasing a false image of the ghost of an absent father.

Grounded

Obama realized, with some encouragement from the clergymen that he was working so closely with during his days as a community organizer in Chicago, that he needed to become more grounded, at least spiritually. He searched for a church that he wanted to join, finally deciding on the Trinity United Church of Christ. This seemingly non-controversial decision later became a potentially polarizing choice and a presidential campaign issue many years later about the church's leader, Reverend Wright.

Obama also realized during this time of his life that he needed to become affiliated with a church. He was working with clergymen every day, and they frequently asked him what church he attended. He joined the Trinity United Church of Christ on the South Side, drawn to this congregation largely in part because of its charismatic spiritual leader, Reverend Doctor Jeremiah A. Wright Jr., who was interested in the African roots of Christianity. The church's motto is "unashamedly black and unapologetically Christian." The title of Obama's second book, *The Audacity of Hope*, is based on a sermon by Reverend Wright, but the book focuses on different ideals than that of the more radical clergyman. Although Obama stayed close to Reverend Wright for many years (even being married by him), during his later political years, Wright became too radical in his views for Obama to publically continue to support him, and Obama distanced himself from Wright to neutralize their relationship as a campaign issue.

After three years trying to help the people from the South Side of Chicago, Obama began to realize that the change that people needed could not come at the community level, but must be achieved by people in positions of authority. He was accepted to Harvard Law School and left these Chicago neighborhoods, vowing to return someday to continue to help these people. He kept this promise, returning many times during and after his graduation from Harvard Law School and never forgetting the people he had set out to help.

Before heading off to Harvard in another newly purchased used car—this time, a bright yellow Datsun 210 hatchback bought for $500 from a Chicago police officer—he went on a pilgrimage to his father's native Kenya, a trip he chronicled in *Dreams of My Father*. He arrived at Harvard at the age of 27 in the fall of 1988. He was somewhat different from most of the preppy first-year law students arriving from other Ivy League colleges. He had a more experienced, worldly attitude and appearance in his leather bomber jacket and jeans, and he smoked cigarettes. He was also only one of a handful of minority students among the future elite of business, legal, and political leaders beginning their law school education at one of the most prestigious legal institutions in the country.

Obama immediately distinguished himself at Harvard in another way, even beyond his appearance and past. Most first-year law students were eager to debate legal points and principles, insisting on getting their viewpoint heard even at the expense of not hearing the merits of the other person's argument. Obama approached legal debate from a different perspective. He instead preferred to listen to the other's viewpoint, ask for clarification and rationale for their position, and try to find a middle ground. When he spoke, people listened. He often made a point that others would have liked to but lacked the confidence to do so, particularly on racial issues. During his years at Harvard, Obama was studious and socialized little, making most of his friends in class. He was unusually confident and self-assured, even for a Harvard Law student. At the end of his first year, classmates convinced him to apply for the *Harvard Law Review*. He nearly missed the deadline to send in his application because of car problems and needed to talk his way to the front of the line at the post office to meet the noon postmark application requirement.

Obama was a member of the Black Law Students Association but was less confrontational than many of its members, typically preferring to discuss and debate issues important to students and faculty. In early 1990, when the presidency of the *Harvard Law Review* was to be decided, Obama reluctantly agreed to submit his name for candidacy— one of nineteen other contenders. Other editors who were not candidates decided the election through a process of debate and process of elimination. Obama was eventually elected, becoming the first African-American president of the *Harvard Law Review*.

Historic

The election of Obama to president of the *Harvard Law Review* in 1990, as the first black to hold this position in its more than 100-year history, was the first indication of just how historic his life would be. Being elected president of the review, considered the highest student position at the *Harvard Law Review* by the other editors, was a significant accomplishment and thrust Obama into the national spotlight, but it was only an indication of what was to come. However, he did not take the traditional route of many others holding this position by going on to serve as a clerk for a judge on the Federal Court of Appeals for a year or then as a clerk for an associate justice of the Supreme Court. Instead, Obama at the time said he planned to spend two or three years in private law practice and then return to Chicago to re-enter community work, either in politics or in local organizing—exactly what he did.

He served as editor for two semesters, working 50–60 hours reviewing hundreds of articles on subjects from corporate law to racial bias. He was clearly a liberal but was able to avoid alienating conservatives by not seeming to take sides on issues.

However, Obama at the time might still not have appreciated his true potential. He wrote *Dreams of My Father* at the urging of a publisher after graduating from Harvard Law School and gaining national notoriety as the first black editor of the *Harvard Law Review*. It seems apparent that he still did not even imagine that he would ever have realistic presidential hopes at the time he penned this candid memoir. He later said that he described his use of drugs as a youth in the book to illustrate how frustrated young people sometimes become during their lives about things they feel that they cannot control. Fortunately for Obama and our nation, he learned that he could do something about these frustrations eventually by seeking political office where he could make a difference. *Dreams of My Father* had an initial run of 15,000 books but fell out of print, that is, until his electrifying 2004 keynote speech at the Democratic National Convention, which propelled it to a national best seller.

During one of his summers at Harvard, Obama returned to Chicago where he worked as a summer associate at the prestigious law firm of Sidley & Austin. His mentor was a first-year associate, Michelle Robinson, a Princeton and Harvard Law graduate that he later married in 1992. Michelle reportedly resisted Barack's initial interest in her but obviously changed her mind. One thing Michelle did to find out more about her suitor at the time was to arrange for him to play basketball with her brother, who now is a college basketball coach. Obama apparently measured up in this "court test."

Sometimes, we seem to set out in our lives, purposely correcting deficiencies we saw in our parents, both in their choices and in their lives. Barack Obama and his wife Michele have created a stable and constant family unit much different from what he experienced growing up. Obama describes their family life this way: "We've created stability for our kids that my mom didn't do for us. My choosing to put down roots in Chicago and marry a woman who is rooted in one place probably indicates a desire for stability that maybe I was missing." Obviously, it was no accident that strength and stability were characteristics that Obama viewed as important in a spouse. Strong women have been a dominant force in Obama's life, from his mother to his grandmother to his wife Michelle, a Harvard Law School graduate and business executive while raising two young daughters, Sasha and Malia.

Obama returned to Chicago in 1991 after graduating from Harvard Law School, turning down countless offers with many prestigious law firms to become a public interest and civil rights lawyer working on cases involving voter rights, employment discrimination, and low-income housing. He also taught constitutional law and a seminar on civil rights at the University of Chicago Law School, where he enjoyed high ratings from students attending his classes.

Inspiring

Obama wrote an inspiring autobiographical book, *Dreams of My Father*, shortly after graduating from Harvard Law School. This book chronicled his journey as a young African-American boy growing up in both distant and familiar lands, struggling to find his identity and ultimately finding his *voice* to eventually inspire an entire nation, and even the world, that your hopes and dreams can come true, no matter how improbable they might seem early on.

Defining Moments

Obama said in an interview in 2000 with the *Chicago Reader*, "I'm like a salmon swimming upstream in the South Side of Chicago. At every juncture in my life I could have taken the path of least resistance but much higher pay." Just think about what motivated Obama to forgo much more lucrative career opportunities to serve the community and society. During his early adulthood, he went from struggling to find a job that barely paid him enough money to survive to having the opportunity to work in virtually any law firm in the country after graduating from Harvard Law School. Obama obviously had a vision of where he wanted to go in life, and following the traditional pathways was not how he saw himself reaching his goals. Think about the vision you have for yourself in life, regardless of where you are now along the journey. Are you making the right decisions to direct you toward your life's goals?

CHAPTER 4

First Attempts

At the urging of friends and colleagues, Obama entered politics for the first time in 1995, believing that public service was the best way to bring about social change. He won the state senator race for Illinois' 13th District, which includes Hyde Park, the South Side, and the University of Chicago, over incumbent Alice Palmer who had decided to run for a congressional seat but lost in the primary. Palmer asked Obama to step aside, so she could regain her position, but he refused, even challenging the authenticity of signatures she had obtained to re-enter the race.

When the people close to him told him that he was getting too intense and serious, he took up golf and played in a bipartisan poker game with other legislators. He, of course, continued to play basketball, a constant in his life. As a state senator, Obama chaired the Public Health and Welfare Committee. He worked on many social justice issues, including federal welfare reform. He sponsored a bill for the state to share its data on the welfare program with researchers. He also worked on the issue of curbing racial profiling, advocated expanded health insurance coverage for the poor, and sponsored a bill to require videotaping of police interrogations in homicide cases. He was known as not being swayed by public opinion polls, but was also practical. He got things done by bringing both sides together to talk to try to find common ground as the basis of agreement. Obama quoted the late Illinois Senator Paul Simon that Americans want politicians who can "disagree without being disagreeable."

Just

Obama offered a different alternative to the traditional political candidate. He was honest and told the truth, not afraid of admitting who he was or talking about his past. He believed in doing what was right and had nothing he was trying to hide. He was fair with the people with whom he dealt and respected people challenging him, even during difficult campaigns that could get rough and personal at times.

Obama unsuccessfully ran for a seat in the U.S. House of Representatives in 2000, as he challenged the Democratic incumbent, Bobby Rush, a former Black Panther with connections to many blacks in Chicago. Obama entered the race against the advice of friends and colleagues who thought the timing was not right and that it was the wrong race for him to enter national politics. Obama's campaign was underfunded, lacked support from people in political power, and he drew criticism for being too connected to whites and too Ivy League. He dressed in a suit and tie, rather than more casually as he did during his later successful presidential campaign. Rush portrayed Obama as being "the candidate of Hyde Park intellectuals and white liberals." He also mocked him as an "educated fool." Some of his supporters believed he had to pay this price for his support outside the black neighborhoods. Obama has been described during this early campaign as stiff and uncomfortable during campaign appearances, emphasizing his Ivy League Harvard education and not connecting with black voters. His body language during campaign events even seemed to show how frustrated and impatient he was at times at events he attended. His opponents also characterized him as not being black enough for the South Side and a white man in blackface.

The tragic death of Rush's son, killed in a robbery just months before the election, resulted in a wave of sympathy for Rush with voters, even forcing Obama to suspend his campaign for a time. During the campaign, one of Obama's daughters also became sick during an annual Christmas family vacation to Hawaii, delaying his return to Springfield and causing him to miss a critical vote on crime that came up earlier than expected. Missing this vote resulted in more bad press and criticism against his campaign and him. Obama failed to raise enough money during the campaign and was nearly helpless, as the primaries neared with Rush receiving the support of then President Bill Clinton on black radio station ads. Obama was soundly defeated in the primaries by a 60–31 percent vote and went back to his state senate seat, frustrated about his future in politics.

The loss was emotional for Obama. In his second book, *The Audacity of Hope*, he writes, "It's impossible not to feel at some level as if you have been personally repudiated by the entire community, that you don't quite have what it takes and that everywhere you do the word 'loser' is flashing though people's minds."

At the age of 38, Obama was returning to a Republican-led state senate in Springfield. He even thought about getting out of politics, his wife even pressuring him to find a more stable, better paying career. He considered becoming president of the Joyce Foundation, a Chicago organization providing support for the environment, schools, and poor, as well as working to reduce crime in Chicago, and of which Obama was on the board of directors at the time. The job paid well, was close to home, and supported his interests, but he would have had to leave the state senate if he were to take the job. He also considered other alternatives, such as going back to practicing law or teaching law school full time. Thoughts of saving money for his daughters' education and buying a better home weighed heavily on his and Michelle's minds at the time.

Nevertheless, his interest in politics could not be extinguished that easily. He felt destined for bigger things. He decided to remain in the state senate and bide his time for opportunity to come his way. He felt he had learned a great deal from his defeat and would be all the wiser the next time he decided to run again. As one colleague, former Congressman Abner J. Mikva, described him, "a very apt student of his own mistakes." This time, he would plan better, create a better organization with the right people working for him, and lay a foundation to build on during the long campaign ahead. He also looked introspectively and examined how he came across to the public. He worked at appearing less intellectual and professorial and more able to connect with voters, to be himself, more like the community organizer he was in his early days in Chicago. He tried to relax the audiences he addressed, and perhaps himself, with self-deprecating wit, saying, "The first thing people ask me is how did you get that name 'Obama,' although they don't always pronounce it right. Some people call it 'Alabama'; some say 'Yo Mamma.' I got my name from Kenya where my father is from; I got my accent from Kansas, where my mother's from," he often explained.

Knowledgeable

Obama offered more than just inspiring speeches and a fresh image to America; he was also intelligent. He could speak intelligently on the issues and debate effectively with more experienced politicians, proving his command of the current issues at hand. He was the "real thing" regarding becoming

a legitimate presidential candidate, bringing to the party all
the attributes and abilities required to attract supporters and
convince the country that he was the best candidate for the job.

Obama learned from this defeat that it was not enough
to believe that you are the best qualified for the job; you need
to have influential people supporting you, which he did not
have in the past. He did not make this same mistake in his
future bids for political office. Obama knew that building
relationships was important in politics. He worked hard to
build these types of positive relationships with lawmakers in
the rural areas of Illinois and from different environments
than Chicago, seeking people of different backgrounds and
generations. These relationships helped him throughout
his political career in Illinois. He realized that having
powerful political friends was also important. He cultivated a
relationship with a powerful Democratic state senate leader,
Emil Jones, a former Chicago sewer inspector from the South
Side, whom Obama called his "political godfather," and who
would be influential in his next political campaign.

Literate

Besides graduating from Columbia University and Harvard
Law School, Barack Obama has written two best-selling
books about his life, *Dreams of My Father: A Story of Race
and Inheritance*, published first in 1995; and *The Audacity of
Hope: Thoughts on Reclaiming the American Dream*, published
In 2006. He writes most of his own speeches, and he is well
respected for not only his oratory skills, but also the content
of his speeches mixed with historical references, symbolism,
and emotional appeal. His keynote speech at the Democratic
National Convention in 2004 is considered one of the great
convention speeches in history, because of not only Obama's
stirring delivery but also the speech itself, almost entirely
written by him.

Obama's literary abilities were also financially profitable to him as well. Obama's personal wealth increased following the speech. Before running for the U.S. Senate in 2004, he reported just over $200,000 in taxable income contrasted to $1.6 million in 2005, $983,826 in 2006, and more than $4.2 million in household income in 2007 because of the sharp increase in sales of his book after his sudden rise to fame.

In October 2002, Obama told an antiwar rally in Chicago, "I don't oppose all wars. What I am opposed to is a dumb war. What I am opposed to is a rash war … I know that even a successful was against Iraq will require a U.S. occupation of underdetermined length, at undetermined cost with undetermined consequences." This position served him well, particularly against future presidential contenders who voted for the unpopular war—even Democratic rival Hillary Clinton.

Defining Moments

Think about Obama's description of how he felt after being so soundly defeated in the second political race in his life. Imagining such a talented and appealing person ever feeling so insecure and rejected is hard. Compare this time in Obama's life with later moments, such as when he spoke at the 2004 Democratic Convention, after winning the Iowa Caucus, accepting the Democratic nomination for president, or on election night. Life is full of failures and victories. How you respond to setbacks and disappointment, and what you learn, can be important elements in later turning failure to victory.

CHAPTER 5

Finding the Formula for Success

Obama did not give up. Two years later, he decided to run for U.S. senator to fill retiring Republican Peter Fitzgerald's seat. Many did not believe that he could win, even though his support base was growing. He was able to raise $6 million in campaign funds, enough to buy television ads enabling him to introduce himself to a broader constituency in this still highly contested political battle. Obama's media appeal paid off. This broader media exposure attracted more campaign money, and he won the primary and had the funding needed for the general election. Another big break came when Obama's Republican opponent, Jack Ryan, became involved in a sex scandal, causing him to withdraw from the race.

Meticulous

People close to him know Obama as a meticulous planner, evident early in his career as a community organizer in Chicago. He meticulously planned events, especially when involving political or government representatives to ask for their support or endorsement of an initiative. This attention to detail also proved invaluable during his later campaigns, ensuring that everything needing to be attended to was taken care of in advance. His staff knew him as "No Drama Obama," meaning that he wanted every detail taken care of, so there would not be any reason to panic or have dramatic moments during critical times in the campaign. He ran a buttoned-up, disciplined campaign in which embarrassing leaks to the press were virtually nonexistent.

As a legislator, he was known as a practical, progressive thinker on issues. Senator Obama's legislative interests included working for families, public education, healthcare, economic growth, job creation, and he is strongly pro-choice and favors universal healthcare. He learned to be more comfortable in his role as a politician, balancing candor and hope in his message to voters. "Obama tells you the hard truths, and other politicians, particularly from Chicago, they tend to tell you what they think you want to hear," said a supporter in his home state of Illinois. "Barack's got something different."

Natural

Obama has a natural appeal, as he usually appears confident and comfortable with himself. However, this naturalness was not always so apparent. In the only political race in which he lost, when running for U.S. Congress in 2000 against an incumbent, Obama was criticized for being impatient, elitist, even as an intellectual snob. His opponent called him an "educated fool." However, Obama learned to present himself more naturally. He consciously tried to be more appealing to the public and more engaging with people, and he was highly successful in re-introducing himself as a natural politician who could relate to a wide variety of voters.

The Big Break

The big break, the one that thrust him into national attention, was an invitation from John Kerry's 2004 presidential campaign to be the keynote speaker at the Democratic National Convention that summer at Boston's Fleet Center on July 27, 2004. They had heard that Obama was a polished speaker, and they wanted someone who would represent the party's diversity. He had been asked the month before to give the Democrats' response to one of President Bush's weekly radio addresses, providing Obama with one of his first opportunities to showcase his oratory skills to a national audience.

Although the radio address was considered a success, hitting all the Democratic themes, it still seemed obvious that someone else had written the speech for Obama, which was the case. Instead of having his aides, including his media advisor David Axelrod and chief press aide Robert Gibbs, he was encouraged to write the drafts of the speech.

He wrote the speech's first drafts in hotel rooms, as he traveled during his campaign for U.S. Senate, with most of it accepted by the Kerry people, who were impressed with its candor, authenticity, and the story he had to tell. Most of all, Obama delivered it with his now famous oratorical skill that, later in his presidential campaign, become his greatest strength as a political candidate. This part came naturally to Obama. He had been less effective communicating one-on-one during his years in the Illinois state senate but learned to listen more attentively to others, to understand their issues, and to empathize with their hopes, dreams, and needs. He used his diverse background and experiences to relate to people from all lifestyles. These acquired skills also served him well during his presidential campaign.

Opportunistic

Sometimes, you need to create your own opportunities in life, and Obama learned to take advantage of situations, as they came his way. During his first political contest for Illinois State Senate, incumbent Alice Palmer decided to run for U.S. Congress but lost in the primary and asked Obama to step aside in the race to allow her to remain in her position. However, Obama refused and successfully challenged the authenticity of signatures petitioning her to re-enter the race.

Obama most certainly seized the opportunity presented to him to present the Keynote Address at the 2004 Democratic National Convention, which significantly changed his future and that of the country.

Keynote Address at the 2004 Democratic National Convention

July 27, 2004

On behalf of the great state of Illinois, crossroads of a nation, land of Lincoln, let me express my deep gratitude for the privilege of addressing this convention. Tonight is a particular honor for me because, let's face it, my presence on this stage is pretty unlikely. My father was a foreign student, born and raised in a small village in Kenya. He grew up herding goats, went to school in a tin-roof shack. His father, my grandfather, was a cook, a domestic servant.

But my grandfather had larger dreams for his son. Through hard work and perseverance my father got a scholarship to study in a magical place: America, which stood as a beacon of freedom and opportunity to so many who had come before. While studying here, my father met my mother. She was born in a town on the other side of the world, in Kansas. Her father worked on oil rigs and farms through most of the Depression. The day after Pearl Harbor, he signed up for duty, joined Patton's army and marched across Europe. Back home, my grandmother raised their baby and went to work on a bomber assembly line. After the war, they studied on the GI Bill, bought a house through FHA, and moved west in search of opportunity.

And they, too, had big dreams for their daughter, a common dream, born of two continents. My parents shared not only an improbable love; they shared an abiding faith in the possibilities of this nation. They would give me an African name, Barack, or "blessed," believing that, in a tolerant America, your name is no barrier to success. They imagined me going to the best schools in the land, even though they weren't rich, because in a generous America you don't have to be rich to achieve your potential. They are both passed away now. Yet, I know that, on this night, they look down on me with pride.

I stand here today, grateful for the diversity of my heritage, aware that my parents' dreams live on in my precious daughters. I stand here knowing that my story is part of the larger American story, that I owe a debt to all of those who came before me, and that, in no other country on earth, is my story even possible. Tonight, we gather to affirm the greatness of our nation, not because of the height of our skyscrapers, or the power of our military, or the size of our economy. Our pride is based on a very simple premise, summed up in a declaration made over two hundred years ago, "We hold these truths to be self-evident, that all men are created equal. That they are endowed by their Creator with certain inalienable rights. That among these are life, liberty, and the pursuit of happiness."

That is the true genius of America, a faith in the simple dreams of its people, the insistence on small miracles. That we can tuck in our children at night and know they are fed and clothed and safe from harm. That we can say what we think, write what we think, without hearing a sudden knock on the door. That we can have an idea and start our own business without paying a bribe or hiring somebody's son. That we can participate in the political process without fear of retribution, and that our votes will he counted—or at least, most of the time.

This year, in this election, we are called to reaffirm our values and commitments, to hold them against a hard reality and see how we are measuring up, to the legacy of our forbearers, and the promise of future generations. And fellow Americans—Democrats, Republicans, Independents—I say to you tonight: we have more work to do. More to do for the workers I met in Galesburg, Illinois, who are losing their union jobs at the Maytag plant that's moving to Mexico, and now are having to compete with their own children for jobs that pay seven bucks an hour. More to do for the father I met who was losing his job and choking back tears, wondering how he would pay $4,500 a month for the drugs his son needs without the health benefits he counted on. More to do for the young woman in East St. Louis, and thousands more like her, who has the grades, has the drive, has the will, but doesn't have the money to go to college.

Don't get me wrong. The people I meet in small towns and big cities, in diners and office parks, they don't expect government to solve all their problems. They know they have to work hard to get ahead and they want to. Go into the collar counties around Chicago, and people will tell you they don't want their tax money wasted by a welfare agency or the Pentagon. Go into any inner city neighborhood, and folks will tell you that government alone can't teach kids to learn. They know that parents have to parent, that children can't achieve unless we raise their expectations and turn off the television sets and eradicate the slander that says a black youth with a book is acting white. No, people don't expect government to solve all their problems. But they sense, deep in their bones, that with just a change in priorities, we can make sure that every child in America has a decent shot at life, and that the doors of opportunity remain open to all. They know we can do better. And they want that choice.

In this election, we offer that choice.
Our party has chosen a man to lead us
who embodies the best this country has to
offer. That man is John Kerry. John Kerry
understands the ideals of community, faith,
and sacrifice, because they've defined his life.
From his heroic service in Vietnam to his
years as prosecutor and lieutenant governor,
through two decades in the United States
Senate, he has devoted himself to this country.
Again and again, we've seen him make tough
choices when easier ones were available. His
values and his record affirm what is best in us.

John Kerry believes in an America
where hard work is rewarded. So, instead of
offering tax breaks to companies shipping
jobs overseas, he'll offer them to companies
creating jobs here at home. John Kerry
believes in an America where all Americans
can afford the same health coverage our
politicians in Washington have for themselves.
John Kerry believes in energy independence,
so we aren't held hostage to the profits of oil
companies or the sabotage of foreign oil fields.
John Kerry believes in the constitutional
freedoms that have made our country the
envy of the world, and he will never sacrifice
our basic liberties nor use faith as a wedge to
divide us. And John Kerry believes that in a
dangerous world, war must be an option, but
it should never be the first option.

A while back, I met a young man named
Shamus at the VFW Hall in East Moline,
Illinois. He was a good-looking kid, six-two

or six-three, clear-eyed, with an easy smile. He told me he'd joined the Marines and was heading to Iraq the following week. As I listened to him explain why he'd enlisted, his absolute faith in our country and its leaders, his devotion to duty and service, I thought this young man was all any of us might hope for in a child. But then, I asked myself: Are we serving Shamus as well as he was serving us? I thought of more than 900 service men and women, sons and daughters, husbands and wives, friends and neighbors, who will not be returning to their hometowns. I thought of families I had met who were struggling to get by without a loved one's full income, or whose loved ones had returned with a limb missing or with nerves shattered, but who still lacked long-term health benefits because they were reservists. When we send our young men and women into harm's way, we have a solemn obligation not to fudge the numbers or shade the truth about why they're going, to care for their families while they're gone, to tend to the soldiers upon their return, and to never ever go to war without enough troops to win the war, secure the peace, and earn the respect of the world.

Now, let me be clear. We have real enemies in the world. These enemies must be found. They must be pursued, and they must be defeated. John Kerry knows this. And just as Lieutenant Kerry did not hesitate to risk his life to protect the men who served with him in Vietnam, President Kerry will not hesitate one moment to use our military might to keep

America safe and secure. John Kerry believes in America. And he knows it's not enough for just some of us to prosper. For alongside our famous individualism, there's another ingredient in the American saga.

A belief that we are connected as one people. If there's a child on the south side of Chicago who can't read, that matters to me, even if it's not my child. If there's a senior citizen somewhere who can't pay for her prescription and has to choose between medicine and the rent, that makes my life poorer, even if it's not my grandmother. If there's an Arab American family being rounded up without benefit of an attorney or due process, that threatens my civil liberties. It's that fundamental belief—I am my brother's keeper, I am my sister's keeper—that makes this country work. It's what allows us to pursue our individual dreams, yet still come together as a single American family. "E pluribus unum." Out of many, one.

Yet even as we speak, there are those who are preparing to divide us, the spin masters and negative ad peddlers who embrace the politics of anything goes. Well, I say to them tonight, there's not a liberal America and a conservative America—there's the United States of America. There's not a black America and white America and Latino America and Asian America; there's the United States of America. The pundits like to slice-and-dice our country into Red States and Blue States; Red States for Republicans, Blue States for

Democrats. But I've got news for them too. We worship an awesome God in the Blue States, and we don't like federal agents poking around our libraries in the Red States. We coach Little League in the Blue States and have gay friends in the Red States. There are patriots who opposed the war in Iraq and patriots who supported it. We are one people, all of us pledging allegiance to the stars and stripes, all of us defending the United States of America.

In the end, that's what this election is about. Do we participate in a politics of cynicism or a politics of hope? John Kerry calls on us to hope. John Edwards calls on us to hope. I'm not talking about blind optimism here—the almost willful ignorance that thinks unemployment will go away if we just don't talk about it, or the health care crisis will solve itself if we just ignore it. No, I'm talking about something more substantial. It's the hope of slaves sitting around a fire singing freedom songs; the hope of immigrants settling out for distant shores; the hope of a young naval lieutenant bravely patrolling the Mekong Delta; the hope of a millworker's son who dares to defy the odds; the hope of a skinny kid with a funny name who believes that America has a place for him, too. The audacity of hope!

In the end, that is God's greatest gift to us, the bedrock of this nation; the belief in things not seen; the belief that there are better days ahead. I believe we can give our middle

class relief and provide working families with a
road to opportunity. I believe we can provide
jobs to the jobless, homes to the homeless,
and reclaim young people in cities across
America from violence and despair. I believe
that as we stand on the crossroads of history,
we can make the right choices, and meet the
challenges that face us. America!

Tonight, if you feel the same energy I do,
the same urgency I do, the same passion I do,
the same hopefulness I do— if we do what
we must do, then I have no doubt that all
across the country, from Florida to Oregon,
from Washington to Maine, the people will
rise up in November, and John Kerry will be
sworn in as president, and John Edwards will
be sworn in as vice president, and this country
will reclaim its promise, and out of this long
political darkness, a brighter day will come.
Thank you, and God bless you.

Defining Moments

There is little doubt that if Obama had not been given the
opportunity to address the Democratic National Convention
that July night in 2004 that he might never have been elected
president of the United States. He took full advantage of this
opportunity of a lifetime by not only writing an inspiring
speech, but also delivering it in a manner that made everyone
take notice of what he had to say. This event was different
from when Obama could not get credentials to attend the
2000 Democratic Convention or had to ask a car rental
agency to overlook unpaid balances on his credit card to get
to the convention. In just four years, he became an overnight
sensation, and immediately, he was thrust into the national

limelight. Obama capitalized on his unique background, experiences, talents, and abilities to cause this phenomenal event to occur. You do not usually get many opportunities to make a significant difference in your life. What have been those moments in your life, and how did you respond? What future opportunities do you envision coming your way in the future that you can make a difference in your life, and how can you prepare yourself for them?

CHAPTER 6

Capitalizing on Success

Personable

Obama has the great ability to relate to different people on a personal level. He can appeal to a diverse spectrum of people partly because of the diversity of his background, but also because of his personality. He immediately puts people at ease with his smile and graciousness. His interest in others comes across as sincere and genuine. He connects with others on a personal level in his speeches and writings—a level that few politicians can achieve.

Following the speech, Barack Obama became an overnight sensation. He was able to handle his newly attained status of a political phenomenon, taking on nearly immediate "rock star" status, seeming unaffected by this sudden national attention. Some worried how Obama would react to this rush of adulation suddenly thrust on him. "I've been blessed with a calm, steady temperament and am someone who reminds myself that it's never as good as it seems and never as bad as it seems," Obama said about himself at the time. He offered a different alternative to the typical stereotypic political candidate. Others worried if he could appeal to broad enough spectrums of voters to be a legitimate presidential candidate. He said in response to the historic nature of his candidacy and the prospect of becoming just the fifth African-American senator in U.S. history and only the third to be popularly elected, "I am rooted in the African-American community, but I am not limited by it."

Quintessential

Receiving the Democratic Party's nomination over Hillary Clinton was no easy feat, nor was his decisive victory over John McCain, a well-respected Republican and national hero. However, Obama was to become the quintessential political candidate during the 2008 campaign, doing just about everything right in his bid to become the 44th president of the United States. At first, he was even an unlikely candidate for many reasons, not the least of which was that he was African-American. Nevertheless, he masterfully designed a political campaign built on his strengths and innovative approaches such as using the Internet to raise campaign funds. He united people together with a theme of "Yes We Can" and on the promise of change for the better in the future.

Obama immediately became a media sensation, appearing on the covers of many prominent national magazines. He was part of a new generation of black politicians who did not rise through the civil rights movement or churches, as did former Democratic presidential hopeful Jesse Jackson. He was more a part of the system, a product of white institutions including Ivy League schools. He was less confrontational and more conciliatory. Race was important to him, but not his main theme or message, which helped Obama attract a more diverse base of political support if even at the expense of some black supporters. He was less Al Sharpton, the minister and civil rights activist and 1994 presidential candidate, and more like Bill Cosby's Cliff Huxtable with whom both blacks and non-blacks could identify,, in sharp contrast to most other black leaders of the past generation whose focus was more on the problems of black Americans than the problems of America.

With a campaign motto of "Yes We Can" and media consultant, David Axelrod, who had spent decades working in Chicago politics, he won the 2004 Illinois Senate race by 70 percent and speculation about a possible 2008 presidential bid began to surface.

Rhetoric

Obama's rhetorical skills turned him into an overnight sensation following his Keynote Address at the Democratic National Convention in 2004 in Boston, immediately transforming him from a little known state senator to a national political figure. His great rhetorical abilities distinguished him from the other candidates throughout the 2008 campaign. He gave soaring speeches filled with hope and promise of change that inspired a nation and even the world, drawing massive crowds whenever he spoke. His "Yes We Can" speech was set to music by Will.i.am and viewed by 10 million people on YouTube and received an Emmy Award. Obama also won Best Spoken Word Album Grammy Awards for versions of his books—*Dreams of My Father* and *The Audacity of Hope*.

The nation was immediately drawn to Obama as someone new, different, and, most of all, authentic. In a crowded field of career politicians and Washington insiders, he offered an alternative. David Axelrod realized that this alternative was Obama's greatest attribute as a candidate. Obama had always been open and honest about himself and his unique life. He unapologetically shared all his experiences and frustrations, not only in his books, but also as he campaigned.

He was unafraid to talk about himself. He provided a glimpse into himself that few politicians were willing to risk. Perhaps it was because he did not have any "skeletons" in his past, at least not ones he had not already acknowledged years before in his memoir.

Axelrod realized that voters wanted to know who their candidate was—who was his mother, who was his father, what experiences have shaped his life and his political views to date. Obama brought all these elements to the campaign. George W. Bush's presidential campaigns were successful for much of this same reason, as America knew who he was and where he came from, having had a long and close relationship with his parents and family and watched him grow into a man and politician in his own right. You could just feel how proud his parents would be of him if he would be elected to the job that his father held just a presidential administration before the Clinton era. Obama was beginning to bring this same familiarity and connection to the nation. He was the people's candidate, although still an unlikely choice, being a black man born in Hawaii, raised in Indonesia until the age of 10, and then eventually finding his way to the South Side of Chicago.

Self-deprecating

Despite his considerable natural attributes and talents, Obama still is able not to take himself too seriously. He often described himself as the "skinny kid with a funny name," as he himself reflects on his success that was less than predictable during many times in his life. He also acknowledges that his wife teases him about his big ears.

Chicago politics had also taught Obama just how tough campaigns can become, and he was prepared for the battles he would have to fight along the trail. He wrote in *The Audacity of Hope* that it was in Springfield that he learned "How the game had come to be played: 'I understood politics as a full contact sport, and minded neither the sharp elbows nor the occasional blindsided hits.'"

Tenacious

Obviously, rising to the most powerful position in the world requires tenacity, particularly if you are black, have less political experience than your political candidates do, and have a name that is not recognized and often mispronounced. Obama demonstrated significant tenacity during many difficult times in his life, most notably during his community organizing days in Chicago and later after losing in the primaries for a U.S. congressional seat in 2000. Despite pressures to take a different path in life, he continued to pursue his political aspirations, going on to be elected as a senator from Illinois in 2004. He then received his party's presidential nomination in 2008, despite a field of worthy opponents, not the least of which was Hillary Clinton, the early odds-on favorite to be the party's candidate.

On a chilly February morning in 2007, then U.S. Senator Barack Obama stood before the Illinois Old State Capitol in Springfield, site of Abraham Lincoln's historic speech against slavery, to announce his candidacy for president of the United States. Obama had considerable challenges in his bid to become the next president of the United States. This announcement followed his sudden notoriety mostly achieved because of his Keynote Speech at the Democratic National Convention in 2004, and without which, he probably would not have stood a chance of mounting even a reasonable presidential campaign against more seasoned and better politically connected candidates.

Of course, he was not the only candidate seeking this job. The Democratic field of presidential hopefuls was crowded at the time with the apparent frontrunner being Hillary Clinton, followed by Obama and John Edwards. However, things started to turn because of a rare poor debate performance by Clinton in October of 2007. Her campaign message of "experience" was beginning to falter to Obama's message of "change."

Unconventional

Presidential candidates and nominees were conventionally both male and white. The Democratic presidential primary race of 2008 offered two unconventional candidates. One was a woman, and the other was a black man. Of the two, the woman was perhaps the more conventional of these two unconventional choices. Hillary Clinton was more conventional in the sense that she had more political experience, was a former First Lady, and had more name recognition, at least early in the race. However, Barack Obama offered something different—a change from the status quo. He was the unconventional pick in the Democratic presidential primary race and in the presidential election, as he faced a well-established Republican opponent, John McCain.

The First Victory

The first primary votes are traditionally cast in the Democratic Iowa Caucus in January. Obama won this initial primary and addressed his supporters with the following message:

Thank you, Iowa.

You know, they said this day would never come. They said our sights were set too high. They said this country was too divided; too disillusioned to ever come together around a common purpose.

But on this January night—at this defining moment in history—you have done what the cynics said we couldn't do. You have done what the state of New Hampshire can do in five days. You have done what America can do in this New Year, 2008. In lines that stretched around schools and churches; in small towns and big cities; you came together as Democrats, Republicans and Independents to stand up and say that we are one nation; we are one people; and our time for change has come.

You said the time has come to move beyond the bitterness and pettiness and anger that's consumed Washington; to end the political strategy that's been all about division and instead make it about addition—to build a coalition for change that stretches through Red States and Blue States. Because that's how we'll win in November, and that's how we'll finally meet the challenges that we face as a nation.

We are choosing hope over fear. We're choosing unity over division and sending a powerful message that change is coming to America.

You said the time has come to tell the lobbyists who think their money and their influence speak louder than our voices that they don't own this government, we do; and we are here to take it back.

The time has come for a President who will be honest about the choices and the challenges we face; who will listen to you and learn from you even when we disagree, who won't just tell you what you want to hear, but what you need to know. And in New Hampshire, if you give me the same chance that Iowa did tonight, I will be that president for America.

Thank you.

I'll be a President who finally makes health care affordable and available to every single American the same way I expanded health care in Illinois—by—by bringing Democrats and Republicans together to get the job done.

I'll be a President who ends the tax breaks for companies that ship our jobs overseas and put a middle-class tax cut into the pockets of the working Americans who deserve it.

I'll be a President who harnesses the ingenuity of farmers and scientists and entrepreneurs to free this nation from the tyranny of oil once and for all.

And I'll be a President who ends this war in Iraq and finally brings our troops home; who restores our moral standing; who understands that 9/11 is not a way to scare up votes, but a challenge that should unite America and the world against the common threats of the twenty-first century; common threats of terrorism and nuclear weapons; climate change and poverty; genocide and disease.

Tonight, we are one step closer to that vision of America because of what you did here in Iowa. And so I'd especially like to thank the organizers and the precinct captains; the volunteers and the staff who made this all possible.

And while I'm at it, on "thank you's," I think it makes sense for me to thank the love of my life, the rock of the Obama family, the closer on the campaign trail; give it up for Michelle Obama.

I know you didn't do this for me. You did this—you did this because you believed so deeply in the most American of ideas— that in the face of impossible odds, people who love this country can change it.

I know this—I know this because while I may be standing here tonight, I'll never forget that my journey began on the streets of Chicago doing what so many of you have done for this campaign and all the campaigns here in Iowa—organizing, and working, and fighting to make people's lives just a little bit better.

I know how hard it is. It comes with little sleep, little pay, and a lot of sacrifice. There are days of disappointment, but sometimes, just sometimes, there are nights like this—a night—a night that, years from now, when we've made the changes we believe in when more families can afford to see a doctor; when our children—when Malia and Sasha and your children—inherit a planet that's a little cleaner and safer; when the world sees America differently, and America sees itself as a nation less divided and more united; you'll be able to look back with pride and say that this was the moment when it all began.

This was the moment when the improbable beat what Washington always said was inevitable.

This was the moment when we tore down barriers that have divided us for too long— when we rallied people of all parties and ages to a common cause; when we finally gave Americans who'd never participated in politics a reason to stand up and to do so.

This was the moment when we finally beat back the politics of fear, and doubt, and cynicism; the politics where we tear each other down instead of lifting this country up. This was the moment.

Years from now, you'll look back, and you'll say that this was the moment—this was the place—where America remembered what it means to hope.

For many months, we've been teased, even derided for talking about hope.

But we always knew that hope is not blind optimism. It's not ignoring the enormity of the task ahead or the roadblocks that stand in our path. It's not sitting on the sidelines or shirking from a fight. Hope is that thing inside us that insists, despite all evidence to the contrary, that something better awaits us if we have the courage to reach for it, and to work for it, and to fight for it.

Hope is what I saw in the eyes of the young woman in Cedar Rapids who works the night shift after a full day of college and still can't afford health care for a sister who's ill; a young woman who still believes that this country will give her the chance to live out her dreams.

Hope is what I heard in the voice of the New Hampshire woman who told me that she hasn't been able to breathe since her nephew left for Iraq; who still goes to bed each night praying for his safe return.

Hope is what led a band of colonists to rise up against an empire; what led the greatest of generations to free a continent and heal a nation; what led young women and young men to sit at lunch counters and brave fire hoses and march through Selma and Montgomery for freedom's cause. Hope—hope—is what led me here today— with a father from Kenya; a mother from Kansas; and a story that could only happen in the United States of America. Hope is the bedrock of this nation; the belief that our destiny will not be written for us, but by us; by all those men and women who are not content to settle for the world as it is; who have the courage to remake the world as it should be.

That is what we started here in Iowa, and that is the message we can now carry to New Hampshire and beyond; the same message we had when we were up and when we were down; the one that can change this country brick by brick, block by block, calloused hand by calloused hand—that together, ordinary people can do extraordinary things; because we are not a collection of Red States and Blue States, we are the United States of America; and at this moment, in this election, we are ready to believe again. Thank you, Iowa.

Clinton Briefly Rebounds

Hillary Clinton came back to win in New Hampshire, a contest thought to be won by Obama until she showed a rare glimpse of emotion during a televised interview days before, believed to have garnered her support, especially among women voters. The Clinton campaign seemed to falter in the next few primaries, possibly because of remarks both she and her husband made that potentially lessened her support from African-American voters. The Clinton campaign was running out of money as Super Tuesday approached and had to make personal loans to her campaign. Clinton won the larger states, but Obama continued to win more states and was especially effective in the caucus states largely ignored by the Clinton campaign. Obama did well in states in which younger, affluent, well-educated voters lived and were most receptive to his message and promise for change. Finally, in June, Obama had gained enough delegates to become the presumptive Democratic presidential nominee. Clinton's campaign ended up severely in debt, resulting in her writing off the $13 million she had lent to her campaign.

Vulnerable

Obama can be described as vulnerable in the sense that he was so honest about himself and his past. In his book, *Dreams of My Father*, he showed many things about himself, his family, and even his use of illegal drugs, something that potentially could have been a major problem for a political candidate, particularly one running for the presidency. However, it seems that Obama's vulnerability at the same time made him seem more honest, open, and even likable. He already admitted what others might have accused him of doing, had he not been so open and honest about himself. Perhaps his openness made this potential issue a non-issue as compared to more controversial questions of past presidential candidates such as Bill Clinton who claimed not to have inhaled when experimenting with marijuana in his younger days. During the political races leading to his election as president, perhaps his greatest vulnerability was his relative inexperience as a U.S. senator and politician on a national level.

The Race against McCain

Obama faced the formidable John McCain in the presidential election. McCain came into the race with instant national name recognition, his well-known distinguished military history and experiences as a POW during the Viet Nam War, experience from previous presidential campaigns, the Republican Party's strong endorsement, and the resulting potential for fundraising. However, McCain experienced fundraising problems during 2007, had his campaign manager and campaign chief strategist leave, and began to slump in the polls. McCain responded with his familiar "underdog" strategy that seemed to work well for him again among voters.

By March of 2008, McCain had locked up a majority of delegates and finally became the presumptive Republican nominee for president after many previous unsuccessful attempts during his political lifetime. McCain's campaign surged after the 2008 Republican National Convention with the surprise announcement of running mate, Alaska Governor Sarah Palin. However, this popularity did not last, as Palin's introduction to the media went poorly, and the reactions to her candidacy became increasingly negative. McCain challenged Obama to "Town Hall" debates, a forum in which the Arizona senator was comfortable. However, Obama could effectively relate to the audience, even in these settings, as he was debating foreign affairs—another McCain political strength.

The Republicans tried to attack Obama's character because of his associations with Reverend Jeremiah Wright from his church in Chicago and his reported relationship with Bill Ayers, a controversial activist from the 1960s and '70s and co-founder of the Weather Underground. Obama kept his cool during these attacks delivered mostly by the Republican vice-presidential nominee Sarah Palin. As the economy began to falter in the fall of 2008, the polls again turned more positively toward Obama. His message of change began to resonate, as the Bush administration was held accountable for the brewing financial mess. Even McCain tried, perhaps unsuccessfully, to distance himself from President Bush and his fiscal policies. Obama outspent McCain's campaign by a four-to-one margin. McCain won 46 percent of the nationwide popular vote, compared to Obama's 53 percent.

Worldly

Even as a young boy, Barack Obama was worldlier than his peers were. He not only had lived much of his first 10 years in far off Indonesia, he was much more focused on international events and issues than his friends, which would become a political asset for him later in his life when running for president, as he faced more experienced opponents with more foreign affairs political experience.

Obama rewrote the book on political fundraising forever. From the beginning of the president campaign, even before the primaries began, Obama was raising unprecedented amounts of funds. In January of 2008, rival democratic candidate Hillary Clinton raised $19.7 million, an impressive total for any candidate so early in the campaign. However, Obama raised $36.8 million, the most ever by a Democratic candidate in a primary race. Obama's ability to attract small donations, allowing him to go back to these same donors repeatedly, was beginning to become painfully apparent to his rival Democratic candidates.

Obama decided early to forgo public financing for his campaign to raise many times more than the $85 million he would have received from the public financing system. This campaign funding advantage allowed Obama to attack his political opponents both from the "air and the ground." Obama with surplus funds could attack his opponents in states in which they were leading, forcing them to spend money to defend their leads in these places at the sacrifice of other states where their victory was far less certain. Obama used this strategy against Hillary Clinton in Pennsylvania and extremely effectively against Republican rival John McCain during the presidential campaign. Obama's amazing fundraising ability continued to give him a decided advantage, as he was able to spend campaign money even in what were once strong Republican states. This advantage caused John McCain to spend not only his limited campaign funds, but also his time in these areas to try to hold on to his lead, rather than in other states he needed to gain more support.

Youthful

Barack Obama became the fifth youngest president at the age of 47. Theodore Roosevelt, John F. Kennedy, Bill Clinton, and Ulysses S. Grant, in that order, were younger than Obama when they took the oath of office. Even if he was not the youngest, his youthful appearance, young family, and personality set him apart from other presidential candidates and made him enormously popular with young voters and supporters.

The Internet has also changed campaigning in significant ways. The Internet is always working for the candidate, raising funds, sending out campaign themes and messages, attacking opponents, and reaching out to new demographics of supporters. Campaigns use the help of such online resources as Facebook, sending messages and updates to "friends" almost daily and analyzing Internet searches to find out what was on potential supports' minds, as they looked for information about candidates online.

Defining Moments

Doubtlessly, Obama successfully used the Internet to raise record campaign dollars in a different way than ever before, but also used these new media tools to reach out to younger voters, whom he was already appealing to with his own youth and charisma. He used this new technology in ways never previously contemplated, at least not on a national scale. Think about how this innovative way to attract supporters and campaign funds made such a difference in this presidential election. In what ways can you be more innovative to help you reach your goals in life, following Obama's example?

CHAPTER 7

Election Night

On election night, November 4, 2008, President-Elect Obama addressed 125,000 supporters gathered in Chicago's Grant Park to celebrate his victory and election as the first African-American president of the United States:

> If there is anyone out there who still doubts that America is a place where all things are possible; who still wonders if the dream of our founders is alive in our time; who still questions the power of our democracy, tonight is your answer.
>
> It's the answer told by lines that stretched around schools and churches in numbers this nation has never seen; by people who waited three hours and four hours, many for the very first time in their lives, because they believed that this time must be different; that their voice could be that difference.
>
> It's the answer spoken by young and old, rich and poor, Democrat and Republican,

black, white, Latino, Asian, Native American, gay, straight, disabled and not disabled— Americans who sent a message to the world that we have never been a collection of Red States and Blue States: we are, and always will be, the <u>United</u> States of America.

It's the answer that led those who have been told for so long by so many to be cynical, and fearful, and doubtful of what we can achieve to put their hands on the arc of history and bend it once more toward the hope of a better day.

It's been a long time coming, but tonight, because of what we did on this day, in this election, at this defining moment, change has come to America.

I just received a very gracious call from Senator McCain. He fought long and hard in this campaign, and he's fought even longer and harder for the country he loves. He has endured sacrifices for America that most of us cannot begin to imagine, and we are better off for the service rendered by this brave and selfless leader. I congratulate him and Governor Palin for all they have achieved, and I look forward to working with them to renew this nation's promise in the months ahead.

I want to thank my partner in this journey, a man who campaigned from his heart and spoke for the men and women he grew up with on the streets of Scranton and rode with on that train home to Delaware, the Vice President-Elect of the United States, Joe Biden.

I would not be standing here tonight without the unyielding support of my best friend for the last sixteen years, the rock of our family and the love of my life, our nation's next First Lady, Michelle Obama. Sasha and Malia, I love you both so much, and you have earned the new puppy that's coming with us to the White House. And while she's no longer with us, I know my grandmother is watching, along with the family that made me who I am. I miss them tonight, and know that my debt to them is beyond measure.

To my campaign manager David Plouffe, my chief strategist David Axelrod, and the best campaign team ever assembled in the history of politics—you made this happen, and I am forever grateful for what you've sacrificed to get it done.

But above all, I will never forget who this victory truly belongs to—it belongs to you.

I was never the likeliest candidate for this office. We didn't start with much money or many endorsements. Our campaign was not hatched in the halls of Washington—it began in the backyards of Des Moines and the living rooms of Concord and the front porches of Charleston.

It was built by working men and women who dug into what little savings they had to give five dollars and ten dollars and twenty dollars to this cause. It grew strength from the young people who rejected the myth of their generation's apathy; who left their homes and their families for jobs that offered little pay and less sleep; from the not-so-young people who braved the bitter cold and scorching heat to knock on the doors of perfect strangers; from the millions of Americans who volunteered, and organized, and proved that more than two centuries later, a government of the people, by the people and for the people has not perished from this Earth. This is your victory.

I know you didn't do this just to win an election and I know you didn't do it for me. You did it because you understand the enormity of the task that lies ahead. For even as we celebrate tonight, we know the challenges that tomorrow will bring are the greatest of our lifetime—two wars, a planet in peril, the worst financial crisis in a century. Even as we stand here tonight, we know there are brave Americans waking up in the deserts of Iraq and the mountains of Afghanistan to risk their lives for us. There are mothers and fathers who will lie awake after their children fall asleep and wonder how they'll make the mortgage, or pay their doctor's bills, or save enough for college. There is new energy to harness and new jobs to be created; new schools to build and threats to meet and alliances to repair.

The road ahead will be long. Our climb will be steep. We may not get there in one year or even one term, but America—I have never been more hopeful than I am tonight that we will get there. I promise you—we as a people will get there.

There will be setbacks and false starts. There are many who won't agree with every decision or policy I make as President, and we know that government can't solve every problem. But I will always be honest with you about the challenges we face. I will listen to you, especially when we disagree. And above all, I will ask you join in the work of remaking this nation the only way it's been done in America for two-hundred and twenty-one years—block by block, brick by brick, calloused hand by calloused hand.

What began twenty-one months ago in the depths of winter must not end on this autumn night. This victory alone is not the change we seek—it is only the chance for us to make that change. And that cannot happen if we go back to the way things were. It cannot happen without you.

So let us summon a new spirit of patriotism; of service and responsibility where each of us resolves to pitch in and work harder and look after not only ourselves, but each other. Let us remember that if this financial crisis taught us anything, it's that we cannot have a thriving Wall Street while Main Street suffers— in this country, we rise or fall as one nation; as one people.

Let us resist the temptation to fall back on the same partisanship and pettiness and immaturity that has poisoned our politics for so long. Let us remember that it was a man from this state who first carried the banner of the Republican Party to the White

House—a party founded on the values of self-reliance, individual liberty, and national unity. Those are values we all share, and while the Democratic Party has won a great victory tonight, we do so with a measure of humility and determination to heal the divides that have held back our progress. As Lincoln said to a nation far more divided than ours, "We are not enemies, but friends … though passion may have strained it must not break our bonds of affection." And to those Americans whose support I have yet to earn—I may not have won your vote, but I hear your voices, I need your help, and I will be your President too.

And to all those watching tonight from beyond our shores, from parliaments and palaces to those who are huddled around radios in the forgotten corners of our world – our stories are singular, but our destiny is shared, and a new dawn of American leadership is at hand. To those who would tear this world down—we will defeat you. To those who seek peace and security – we support you. And to all those who have wondered if America's beacon still burns as bright—tonight we proved once more that the true strength of our nation comes not from our the might of our arms or the scale of our wealth, but from the enduring power of our ideals: democracy, liberty, opportunity, and unyielding hope.

For that is the true genius of America— that America can change. Our union can be perfected. And what we have already achieved gives us hope for what we can and must achieve tomorrow.

This election had many firsts and many stories that will be told for generations. But one that's on my mind tonight is about a woman who cast her ballot in Atlanta. She's a lot like the millions of others who stood in line to make their voice heard in this election except for one thing—Ann Nixon Cooper is 106 years old.

She was born just a generation past slavery; a time when there were no cars on the road or planes in the sky; when someone like her couldn't vote for two reasons—because she was a woman and because of the color of her skin.

And tonight, I think about all that she's seen throughout her century in America—the heartache and the hope; the struggle and the progress; the times we were told that we can't, and the people who pressed on with that American creed: Yes we can.

At a time when women's voices were silenced and their hopes dismissed, she lived to see them stand up and speak out and reach for the ballot. Yes we can.

When there was despair in the dust bowl and depression across the land, she saw a nation conquer fear itself with a New Deal, new jobs and a new sense of common purpose. Yes we can.

When the bombs fell on our harbor and tyranny threatened the world, she was there to witness a generation rise to greatness and a democracy was saved. Yes we can.

She was there for the buses in Montgomery, the hoses in Birmingham, a bridge in Selma, and a preacher from Atlanta who told a people that "We Shall Overcome." Yes we can.

A man touched down on the moon, a wall came down in Berlin, a world was connected by our own science and imagination. And this year, in this election, she touched her finger to a screen, and cast her vote, because after 106 years in America, through the best of times and the darkest of hours, she knows how America can change. Yes we can.

America, we have come so far. We have seen so much. But there is so much more to do. So tonight, let us ask ourselves—if our children should live to see the next century; if my daughters should be so lucky to live as long as Ann Nixon Cooper, what change will they see? What progress will we have made?

This is our chance to answer that call. This is our moment. This is our time—to put our people back to work and open doors of opportunity for our kids; to restore prosperity and promote the cause of peace; to reclaim the American Dream and reaffirm that fundamental truth—that out of many, we are one; that while we breathe, we hope, and where we are met with cynicism, and doubt, and those who tell us that we can't, we will respond with that timeless creed that sums up the spirit of a people:

Yes We Can. Thank you, God bless you, and may God Bless the United States of America.

Zealous

Obama was able to energize the country in ways not seen in many years, even decades. His enthusiasm and message of change drew large crowds and legions of supporters wherever he appeared in public. His message of hope and change resonated with millions of Americans looking for a better future, not only for themselves, but also for generations to come.

Defining Movements

Barack Obama's election was a clear defining moment for not only the United States, but also the world. For the first time, an African American had been elected president of the United States. The message is that anything is possible now. President Obama's improbable journey to the White House is proof that the American dream is still alive and that anyone can be anything he or she aspires to be in this world. "A new dawn of American leadership is at hand," Obama said on the eve of the election.

Indeed, a new dawn of leadership has arrived.

References

Adams, Richard. 2007. Barack Obama. *The Guardian*, May 9.

Barack Obama. *Wikipedia*. http://en.wikipedia.org/wiki/ Barack_Obama.

Bernstein, David. 2007. The speech. *Chicago Magazine* (June).

Boss-Bicak, Shira. 2005. Barack Obama '83. *Columbia College Today* (January).

Cadel, Emily. 2008. Obama outshines other candidates in January fundraising. *CQ Today Online News*, February 21.

Calmes, Jackie. 2007. Statehouse yields clues to Obama. *Wall Street Journal*, February 23.

Helman, Scott. 2007. Early defeat launched a rapid political climb. *Boston Globe*, October 12.

Hillary Clinton. *Wikipedia*. http://en.wikipedia.org/wiki/ Hillary_Clinton.

John McCain. *Wikipedia*. http://en.wikipedia.org/wiki/John_ McCain.

Keynote address at the 2004 Democratic national convention. 2004. *Organizing for America,* July 27. http://www. barackobama.com/2004/07/27/keynote_address_at_ the_2004_de.php.

Levenson, Michael, and Saltzman, Jonathan. 2007. At Harvard Law, a unifying voice. *The Boston Globe*, January 28.

Lizza, Ryan. 2007. The agitator: Barack Obama's unlikely political education (alternate link). *New Republic* (March).

Maraniss, David. 2008. Though Obama had to leave to find himself, it is Hawaii that made his rise possible. *Washington Post*, August 22.

McClelland, Edward. 2007. How Obama learned to be a natural. *Salon* (February).

Obama, Barack. 1995, 2004. *Dreams of my father: A story of race and inheritance.* New York: Three Rivers Press.

———. 2006. *The audacity of hope: Thoughts on reclaiming the American dream.* New York: Crown Publishing Group.

Preston, Mark. 2008. Preston on politics: Obama's shock and awe. *CNN Politics.com*, June 24.

Remarks of President-Elect Barack Obama: Election night. 2008. *Organizing for America*, November 4. http:// www.barackobama.com/2008/11/04/remarks_of_ presidentelect_bara.php.

Remarks of Senator Barack Obama: Iowa Caucus night. 2008. *Organizing for America,* January 3. http://www. barackobama.com/2008/01/03/remarks_of_senator_ barack_obam_39.php.

Ripley, Amanda. 2008. The story of Barack Obama's mother. *Time* (April).

Scott, Janny. 2007. A streetwise veteran schooled young Obama. *The New York Times*, September 9.

———. 2007. A member of a new generation, Obama walks a fine line. *International Herald Tribune*, December 28.

Sector, Bob, and McCormick, John. 2007. Portrait of a pragmatist. *Chicago Tribune*, March 30.

Seelye, Katharine Q. 2006. Obama offers more variations from the norm. *New York Times*, October 24. (accessed January4, 2008).

Spellman, Cindy Kerber. 2008. Search and the presidential campaign. *MediaPost's Search Insider* (December).

Tani, Carolyn. 2007. A kid named Barry. *Punahou Bulletin* (Spring).

Wallace-Wells, Benjamin. 2004. The great black hope: What's riding on Barack Obama? *Washington Monthly.com*, November 24.

———. 2007. Obama's narrator. *The New York Times Magazine*, April 1.

Zeleny, Jeff. 2008. Book sales lifted Obama's income in 2007 to a total of $4.2 million. *The New York Times*, April 17.

101 Definitions of Barack Obama

All leaders possess unique leadership characteristics that define their leadership styles and, ultimately, their effectiveness. No single ability or set of characteristics ensures that a leader will be effective in leading others or will even positively influence an organization. What is most important is that a leader demonstrates those characteristics most natural and comfortable to him or her.

President Barack Obama is a complex individual with many different dimensions and characteristics. He is able and comfortable demonstrating any number of different leadership attributes. The following 100 definitions begin to define President Obama and his many different abilities and personal characteristics:

1. **Aggressive**. Leaders such as President Obama must be aggressive in different ways. Being aggressive might mean that the leader acts decisively, challenges others and ideas, or is in the forefront on different issues. Obama was also

very aggressive in his ambitious goal to become president. He did not pay attention to those doubters saying that he did not have enough experience to be elected; instead, he aggressively pursued this goal to its successful completion.

2. **Appealing**. There is no doubt that one of Obama's greatest strengths as leader is how appealing he is to voters and to the public. He attracts people because of his appealing characteristics in his appearance and in his personality and interest in people.

3. **Approachable**. Obama seems more approachable than many other politicians

4. because he seems like someone you have known for a long time. Although the average citizen would not likely ever get the opportunity to be physically near him for security reasons, he still is emotionally approachable in his style and mannerisms that come across even through the media.

5. **Athletic**. President Obama is known for his love of basketball and spends time exercising daily. This athleticism creates a stronger image for President Obama and is something that many people can relate to now and admire him.

6. **Audacity.** Obama's second book is entitled *The Audacity of Hope* and is about his personal views and offers a vision of the future that involves repairing what he believes is a "political process that is broken" and restoring a government that has fallen out of touch with the people.

7. **Authentic**. Obama is generally considered to be the "real thing," meaning that he does not put on

airs or pretend to be something or someone that he is not. He seems very comfortable with himself and consequently helps others feel the same way.

8. **Balanced**. President Obama is a complicated person with many different aspects. He is a unique blend of sophistication and commonness. He holds two degrees from Ivy League schools, yet there were times in his life as a student and young adult when he barely survived economically. Even his heritage is a balance of several different cultures and worlds. This is perhaps why he is so appealing to so many different people.

9. **Bipartisan**. As a politician, Obama has been known for his bipartisan efforts to work with Democrats and Republicans alike to achieve the goals in the best interest of his home state as well as the country as a senator and now president. He has been willing to cross political lines whenever the issue at hand is more important than politics.

10. **Beneficial**. From Obama's early days as a community organizer in Chicago, he has worked for the benefit of those in need. He decided as a young man that he wanted to have a positive impact on others. His work from that time forward has focused on doing beneficial things for the underprivileged and those who are deserving of help.

11. **Calm**. Leaders are often judged by how they react to pressure. Although Obama's experience on the national political scene was somewhat limited prior to his election as president, much could be learned about how he would react under fire, as his political opponents, both from within his party and from the opposition party, tested

his temperament as they attacked his credentials and character during the long campaign process. Obama proved his ability to remain calm under fire, despite efforts to rattle him and make him lose his "cool."

12. **Candid.** Obama wrote in his 1995 memoir, entitled *Dreams of My Father*, very candidly about his life and even that he used drugs during his adolescence. He never apologized or tried to deny any things that he shared about himself in his later years when he began seeking public office. This candidness has helped him be perceived as credible and honest to the public.

13. **Celebrity**. Obama rose almost overnight to celebrity status from a relatively unknown state senator, following his electrifying Keynote Speech at the 2004 Democratic National Convention. He drew "rock star" size crowds during the presidential campaign, and his election as president was followed throughout the world with great anticipation and celebration.

14. **Charismatic**. Obama has charisma. His poise, self-assurance, intelligence, and smile attract people from all lifestyles and backgrounds. This charisma is most apparent when he speaks to crowds of people—the larger, the better. His ability to charm not only crowds, but also supporters on a one-to-one basis, is one of his greatest assets and perhaps distinguished him the most from the other candidates.

15. **Charitable.** Obama and his wife Michelle have contributed their own money to a number of charitable causes, such as AIDS causes in Africa, over the years, but he is charitable in other ways

as well. He has been charitable in his time and concern for the poor and underprovided in this country, working for three years as a community organizer on the South Side of Chicago after graduating from Columbia.

16. **Common**. Barack Obama came from somewhat humble beginnings. His family was not poor, but neither were they upper-class. He learned to understand and relate to people on all levels of society from an early age, especially during his early years living in Indonesia until he was 10 years old and recalling people begging for assistance coming to his mother's home. He also was not afraid to live and work in Chicago's South Side as a community organizer, sometimes in parts of the city that others might have been reluctant to visit, much less live in.

17. **Communicator**. President Obama's greatest leadership strengths are his communication abilities. His campaign speeches drew huge crowds to hear his inspirational words. He is also effective in connecting with people on a personal level, showing interest in all people and their lives, as well as in their issues.

18. **Competitive**. You have to have a competitive spirit to reach the highest political office in the country, and Obama has certainly shown that he is a fierce competitor. He was able to successful compete with the nation's top political candidates during the 2008 primaries and then in the general election, defeating such powerful opponents as Hillary Clinton and John McCain. Early in his political career, during his first race for Illinois state senator, he was asked to step aside in the race

by the incumbent who had earlier decided to seek another political office but lost in the primaries and wanted to return to her former position. Obama not only refused to step aside, but also eventually successfully challenged the authenticity of signatures she had said she received to re-enter the race.

19. **Compromising**. Even as a Harvard law student, Obama was known for his ability to gain compromise during legal debates and arguments. He listens to both sides of the issue and asks clarifying questions to ensure understanding of others' viewpoints, finding ways to bring both sides to some kind of agreement.

20. **Conciliatory**. Obama understands that you cannot always get everything you want, and that at times, you need to agree to what is possible rather than ideal. His early days as a community organizer taught him to help others find ways to get what they needed from the system rather than setting out with unrealistic goals. As a politician, he is known for crossing political lines when necessary to find a way to pass legislation that meets everyone's interests at least in some way.

21. **Credible**. Obama has great credibility with the public because of his honesty, candor, communication abilities, intelligence, and openness about himself. Through his books, we have learned much about his life, feelings, past, and even weaknesses. His openness has allowed the public to feel that they know him and what he is about as a person and ultimately as our president, all of which enhances his credibility as a political figure.

22. Cultural. Obama has lived in a number of different cultures during his lifetime, being raised in both Indonesia and Hawaii. He is also biracial and spent much of his youth living with his white maternal grandparents. These experiences allow him to better understand and appreciate different cultures and be more sensitive to their issues and needs.

23. Dependable. Sometimes, we lead our lives, trying to be what we feel might have been lacking in our upbringing and ensuring that we provide that for our children. Although Obama lived a fascinating life as a youth, he lacked a dependably present parent. He and his wife Michelle have worked hard to provide a dependable family environment for their children, despite their busy and demanding careers.

24. Determined. Obama lost his second political contest when he ran for a U.S. congressional seat in Chicago in 2000, being soundly defeated by the incumbent in the primary election by a margin of 2 to 1. He even considered leaving politics for a more lucrative and stable career. Fortunately, his determination to reach his personal and political goals kept him going forward and not giving up his dreams. Four years later, he ran for a U.S. senate seat from Illinois, which he won by a considerable margin.

25. Diplomatic. Obama learned from a relatively early age the importance of being diplomatic. As a community organizer in Chicago, he helped underprivileged citizens learn to deal diplomatically through the system to get basic needs and problems addressed. He taught them that you would get much farther working with the system rather than against it and that neither anger nor hostility is the way to get your goals accomplished.

26. **Diverse**. Barack Obama is undoubtedly the most diverse president ever to occupy the White House. Born from a black father and white mother in Hawaii, he spent much of his youth living in Indonesia before returning to Hawaii to live with his maternal grandparents and eventually graduate from high school.

27. **Dreamer**. Obama wrote an autobiographical memoir entitled *Dreams of My Father* after graduating from Harvard Law School. The book provides a fascinating glimpse into Obama, chronicling much of his early life and including his hopes for the future, written at a time perhaps before he ever dreamed of becoming president of the United States.

28. **Dynamic**. Obama was thrust on the national political scene in 2004 with a dynamic image, as he addressed the Democratic National Convention in Boston. His powerful oratory skills and message of hope and possibility energized the audience and eventually the nation. He made such a dynamic impact that he immediately became mentioned as a presidential candidate for 2008.

29. **Elegant**. Barack Obama has a certain elegance and grace in his presence and delivery every time he walks into a room or steps before a microphone. His appearance and mannerisms are impeccable and proper. Even when dressing casually, which he often did during the 2008 campaign, he still had

a certain air of elegance, distinguishing him from the other candidates.

30. **Elite.** Although Obama probably would not describe himself as elite, this would have been an apt description of him even before becoming president. Obama held the most elite position possible for any student at Harvard Law School as president of the prestigious *Harvard Law Review.* This distinguished and coveted position typically brought with it offers to work for the most prestigious law firms in the country. However, Obama chose not to pursue the opportunities that this elite position would have afforded and instead pursued a different goal, joining a smaller, less prestigious law firm in Chicago to work as a civil rights lawyer after graduating from Harvard's Law School.

31. **Engaging.** From the time Obama was a young man, he was always known for being personable and social and having an engaging personality. He, later in his life, would be willing to engage in discussions and debates, especially in law school, about issues and topics that others were more reluctant to address. When dealing with others, he is fully engaged and makes people feel that they have his undivided attention.

32. **Ethical.** Barack Obama is one politician who has nothing to hide about his past—something not always so common now. The only things his political opponents could even accuse him of were his relationships with certain controversial individuals, including the Reverend Wright from Obama's church in Chicago, but with whom he had no direct influence. Perhaps his only

indiscretion was his admitted use of drugs as a young man, something that he wrote very openly about in his first book and then readily admits to now, neutralizing this as a potential political issue.

33. Familiar. Obama is the type of public figure that you feel as if you know personally through the media. He does not seem to put on any false pretense or airs and comes across as genuine and familiar. Perhaps his background and heritage are so diverse that everyone can relate to and recognize a part of him.

34. Focused. Although, as a youngster, Obama seemed to lack focus, perhaps because of the many changes he experienced in his life growing up, he later became focused on making a positive difference in the world by first becoming a community organizer in Chicago and then later, after graduating from Harvard Law School, working as a civil rights attorney and later entering politics.

35. Forgiving. Obama does not seem to hold grudges against those who oppose him. He honors his opponents, showing respect for their abilities and understanding the rules of competition. He even appointed his Democratic rival Hillary Clinton to a cabinet position as Secretary of State.

36. Frank. Obama is very frank and honest in his dealings with others. He talks openly about himself and his past, and he does not pull any punches when it comes to dealing with the realities that our nation must face now and in the days to come. This frankness is part of Obama's universal appeal and something that helped him gain the trust and confidence of the voters who elected him as president.

37. **Gracious**. One sign of a great leader is to be gracious in not only defeat, but also victory. Obama graciously acknowledged the skills and contributions of his major political opponents, both John McCain and Hillary Clinton.

38. **Grounded**. Perhaps it is Obama's past, much of it living in very basic surroundings, particularly during his growing-up years in Indonesia, that makes him so grounded in his principles and perspectives today. He has seen firsthand the poverty and despair that people in other parts of the world, as well as in our country, live in now.

39. **Generous**. Barack Obama and his wife have given generously to their favorite charities over the years, including supporting AIDS victims in Africa. However, Obama is generous in other ways as well, not only generously sharing his own personal story, but also in his attention to others less fortunate and disadvantaged in this world. He has given his time generously to help these people, instead of pursuing more lucrative career options readily accessible to him.

40. **Historic**. What Barack Obama accomplished by being elected the first African-American president of the United States is truly an historic accomplishment of unprecedented proportion. He was also the first African-American president of the *Harvard Law Review* and only the third popularly elected black U.S. senator.

41. **Honest**. Obama has read and studied Abraham Lincoln and has obviously emulated many of his

qualities, including honesty. Obama has earned the reputation of being an honest politician, one that you can count on to be truthful and not shy away from telling the truth about himself or his past.

42. **Hopeful**. A major theme for Obama during his campaign to become the 44th president was that of hope for a better future. His message of change resonated to the millions of Americans hoping for a better future, including a healthier economy.

43. **Human**. One thing that can be said about Obama is that he has the same human frailties as anyone else and will be the first to admit them. He is very candid about what he believes to be his weaknesses and even bad habits as a youth. He does not hold himself up on a pedestal as someone who is any better than anyone else is, but rather tries to relate to others, acknowledging his own inadequacies as a human being.

44. **Humble**. In his Keynote Speech at the Democratic National Convention in 2004 thrusting him into the national limelight, Obama humbly said, "Tonight is a particular honor for me because, let's face it, my presence on this stage is pretty unlikely. My father was a foreign student, born and raised in a small village in Kenya. He grew up herding goats, went to school in a tin-roof shack. His father, my grandfather, was a cook, a domestic servant."

45. **Idealistic**. As most politicians, Obama has a vision for a better future for the country. He said on election night, as he addressed a crowd of more than 100,000 and talked about this vision, "This is our moment. This is our time ...." Obama believes

in the ideals he talks about and is willing to work hard to make them become a reality.

46. **Impatient**. In Obama's early political days, he sometimes showed his impatience with the long ordeal that candidates sometimes must go through to be elected to the public office they seek. There are those who recall an impatient, less tolerant Obama on the campaign trail during that time, when both his facial expressions and body language showed his frustration and annoyance during certain political events and debates. However, he learned from these experiences, and he obviously became more patient with the political process in future campaigns.

47. **Inclusive**. Just Obama's presence on the national political scene is proof of this concept of inclusiveness coming of age. Obama himself has focused on including both minorities and women in his political appointments after being elected president, and he is aware of the importance of this inclusiveness.

48. **Innovator**. Obama's presidential campaign rewrote the book on the way to communicate with the country and to raise funds by using the Internet in innovative ways never used before. Obama decided to forgo the limitations of federal funding for smaller individual private donations solicited largely through the internet but greater in total that he would have otherwise received.

49. **Inquisitive**. During his years at Harvard Law School, Obama was known to ask questions about why others would take a particular position, rather than debate with fellow law students. This was unusual for law students who typically focus more

on winning their argument, rather understanding the other person's viewpoint. His genuine interest in others' opinions helped him better articulate and communicate his own position on issues.

50. **Insightful**. Obama's diverse background and experiences have enabled him to have insight into many other people's lives, ideals, expectations, and even dreams. He has used these experiences to gain this insight into others and can better represent their interests in his role as president, perhaps more than any of his predecessors.

51. **Inspiring**. President Obama has inspired millions of people, not only by his improbable journey to the highest political office in the land but by who he is as a person. Obama exemplifies what a leader should be in many ways. He is an example of how we can overcome many negatives we face in life and focus on the right things, as we strive to reach our goals.

52. **Intellectual**. It was apparent from the time that Obama was a young boy that he was intellectually gifted. His mother worried during his younger years living in Indonesia that he was not getting the quality education he deserved and sent him back to Hawaii to live with her parents, so he could attend the Panahou School, an exclusive private school. He would later graduate from two Ivy League schools: Columbia University and Harvard Law School, magna cum laude, where he was elected president of the prestigious *Harvard Law Review*.

53. **Intelligent**. Obama is not only intellectual, but also intelligent—the distinction in this case being that he was able to use his intellectual abilities to

reach ambitious goals, not only for himself, but also for others. He can "think on his feet" and make good decisions and judgments, using his intelligence—something that not everyone with intellectual abilities can do.

54. **Just**. Obama can make fair and impartial decisions based on the facts. He is honest in his opinions and truthful in his responses. Obama's many life experiences perhaps enhance this quality of being just—something that is a very good quality to have in a president.

55. **Kind**. Obama has seen how cruelly humanity can be treated in different parts of the world. These experiences also help him be to be a kinder, more compassionate leader.

56. **Knowledgeable**. During the presidential debates, first with Hillary Clinton and later with Republican presidential nominee, John McCain, Obama demonstrated a good knowledge of foreign affairs as well as national domestic issues, despite his relatively short time serving in the U.S. Senate. He was obviously well read and prepared for these debates and comfortable discussing any issues brought forward. Friends even remember Obama earlier in his life as being very knowledgeable about world events and able to talk knowledgably about many different subjects.

57. **Kidding**. Obama can take a joke about himself from others and is the first to poke fun at himself. He often describes himself growing up as "the skinny kid with a funny name," and he acknowledges that his ears stick out.

58. Liberal. Obama is clearly a Democratic Liberal and was referred to as the most liberal Democrat in the Senate. However, he also is known for his bipartisan efforts to pass legislation that transcends party lines and is in the best interest of the people of this country.

59. Literate. Obama wrote two best-selling books, *Dreams of My Father* and *The Audacity of Hope* before being elected president. After graduating from Columbia University, he worked for about a year as a writer for a business publication in New York. He wrote many of his own speeches, including his Keynote Address at the 2004 Democratic National Convention, considered one of the best speeches ever written for such an occasion. His publishers say that he writes nearly perfect copy, requiring only a minimum of editing.

60. Likable. Obama is a very likable person, one of his greatest strengths as a politician and leader. People have always been drawn to him with his good looks, smile, and his pizzazz, even from the time he was a young boy.

61. Methodical. Obama is known to be very methodical in his planning. This was evident during his days as a community organizer in Chicago when he would meticulously plan for each event he organized, reviewing and rehearsing everything that needed to take place, especially when government officials were invited to presentations of requests for public funding or support.

62. Mobilized. Obama was able to mobilize resources during his presidential campaign in unique and very effective ways, particularly utilizing the

Internet and other electronic media to solicit campaign funds and supporters.

63. **Married.** Barack and Michelle Obama have a strong marriage and family life that serves as a model for couples everywhere. Their devotion for one another is evident every time you see them together.

64. **Narrative.** Obama has won two Grammy Awards for his recordings of his two best-selling books, *Dreams of My Father* and *The Audacity of Hope*.

65. **Nontraditional.** Obama is certainly not your traditional politician or president, for that matter. His groundbreaking achievement of becoming the first African-American president has changed this nation and even the world in many ways.

66. **Outspoken.** Obama is not afraid to speak his mind on issues of importance to him, regardless of politics and expectations. Even in law school, he was known for addressing sensitive topics, such as racial issues, on which others might have been more reluctant to speak out.

67. **Open.** Obama is very open about himself and his life and shares much about himself, not only in his books, but also in his speeches and discussions with others.

68. **Parental.** It is also very evident just how important his role as a parent to his two young daughters is to him every time you see them together or even when he mentions Sasha and Malia.

69. **Personable.** Obama is personable and obviously very comfortable with himself and puts everyone else at ease as a result. He moves easily through

a crowd, connecting in some way with everyone present.

70. **Perspective**. Obama has a good perspective on the issues that this country faces from his own unique life and experiences. He understands, more than any of his predecessors in the White House did, what it means to be a minority in this country and what it takes to be successful, despite the disadvantages that this might create.

71. **Phenomenal**. Obama is a phenomenon. He is an exceptional person with a unique combination of background, personal characteristics, and ability, enabling him to become the man he is now. His phenomenal success in such a short period is further proof of just how exceptional and unique he really is.

72. **Polished.** Although Obama came from relatively humble beginnings, he has a air of polish and sophistication that is not common, even among politicians.

73. **Pragmatic**. Obama understands that there are certain realities existing that limit even the most important objectives from being easily achieved. He has lofty goals but a pragmatic understanding of what is possible to achieve and on what timetable. When faced with the economic crisis that began during the later part of the presidential campaign, Obama promised no quick fixes to a problem that took a long time to develop.

74. **Present**. Obama is definitely present wherever he is. He has a strong presence that gets everyone's attention, not by talking the loudest or being

flashy, but by his natural charisma and engaging personality.

75. **Principled**. Obama has strong personal principles that he lives by every day. He is not a contradiction between his principles and actions. He is a dedicated husband and father and demonstrates the highest of ethical standards as a politician and legislator.

76. **Promising**. Promise has been Obama's strongest message since he announced his candidacy for president. His "Yes We Can" campaign theme resonated with voters who hope for the promise of a better future.

77. **Prowess**. Obama has demonstrated great prowess in just about every endeavor he has undertaken during his lifetime. He was an excellent student in school; made a difference for those he helped as a community organizer; became an effective legislator as a state, and then later U.S., senator; and won the presidential election. He also became a good basketball player, a passion of his, even to the point that he once hoped to become a professional player.

78. **Reflective**. Obama has reflected back on his life in great detail in his best-selling autobiographical book, *Dreams of My Father*. He describes in detail the history of his family, his growing-up years, and his self-discovery about being an African-American man in America.

79. **Respectful**. Obama is respectful of others, perhaps in large part because he knows firsthand what it is like to be different from others. As a young boy growing up in Hawaii, he remembers being one

of only a few blacks in the school he attended and the way other children treated him. Later, in his life in Chicago working on the South Side as a community organizer, he taught citizens that dealing with public officials respectfully is a better way to get the help you are seeking.

80. **Real.** Obama is the real thing. He does not put on pretenses or act any differently, just because he happens to be president of the United States, than he did when he was a relatively unknown state legislator or even back in the days when he struggled to find a job after graduating from college. This realness is one characteristic about Obama that made him most appealing as a presidential candidate.

81. **Savvy**. Obama has a savvy about him that is apparent the moment he enters a room. He connects comfortably with people, putting everyone at ease.

82. **Searching**. Obama spent much of his youth and adolescence searching for his identity, not only as an African American, but also as a person. This was certainly understandable, considering the number of different and even exotic places he was moved to as a child. From about the age of 10 years, he spent much of his youth living with his white maternal grandparents in Hawaii. He only lived one month with his father as a young boy, spending much of the rest of his life trying to understand who is father was and consequently searching for his own identity.

83. **Self-assured**. Obama has always had a self-assurance evident to everyone meeting him. He is

personable and outgoing, attracting everyone to him with his bright smile and self-deprecating wit.

84. **Sensible**. Obama brings a sensibility to politics, bringing issues into focus. He proposes solutions to problems that are practical and reasonably implemented.

85. **Social**. Obama enjoys people, and he has always been surrounded by friends and family. Barack and his wife Michelle have large holiday family gatherings, and he stays in touch with friends from his past.

86. **Strategic**. Obama had a vision of what he wanted from life from the time he was a young adult, although he might not have shared just how ambitious this plan might have been. Obama seemed to realize that forgoing more lucrative career opportunities after graduating from Columbia University could lead to bigger things eventually. His decision to work as a community organizer at that time might have been the most important career move he ever made, establishing a foundation for his later political career that eventually led him to the presidency.

87. **Stylistic**. People are very complimentary about Obama's appearance and style, wearing his clothes well. His wife Michelle has become a fashion icon, regularly setting new trends with every new outfit.

88. **Substantive**. Despite Obama's often unassuming manner, he has many abilities and accomplishments. He graduated from two Ivy League schools including Harvard Law School; he was elected president of the *Harvard Law Review*; he wrote two best-selling autobiographies and

served in the Illinois State Senate; all before being elected president of the United States. These are all significant accomplishments that are evidence of his substantive talents.

89. **Tolerant**. Obama learned tolerance from an early age, as he grew up living in cultures in which he was different from most others. This taught him to be tolerant of people and their attitudes and behaviors.

90. **Tough**. Because of experiences that he sought as a young man, such as becoming a community organizer after graduating from Columbia University, living and working on the South Side of Chicago, and leaving more comfortable surroundings in Hawaii to live as a student in Los Angeles and New York City, Obama learned what it was like to live as a black in urban America. These experiences helped toughen him and make him more resilient.

91. **Trailblazing**. Obama might not have been the first African-American candidate for president, but he is the most successful. Obama's 2008 presidential campaign redefined the way political campaigns would be run in the future by using the Internet to raise campaign funds and support in ways never before tried. Instead of accepting federal campaign funding along with their rules and regulations, Obama's campaign instead relied on private smaller donations, raising significantly more money that his opponents, giving him a significant advantage over them in the primaries and general election.

92. **Teacher**. You learn much just listening to Obama speak about the issues and his vision for the future.

He also taught constitutional law and a seminar on civil rights at the University of Chicago Law School where he enjoyed high student ratings from those attending his classes.

93. Unifier. Obama's goal is to be a bipartisan leader bringing both sides of the political aisle together to bring about the change needed to move the country forward toward a better future. Even back in his days as a Harvard law student, he was known for trying to bring differing people with differing opinions and arguments toward common ground and agreement.

94. Unique. Obama is certainly a unique person, not only because of his biracial heritage, but also because of his early life experiences being raised in Indonesia and Hawaii—not your typical upbringing for anyone, not to mention a president of the United States.

95. Unprecedented. His election as the first African-American president of the United States was certainly an unprecedented event. However, Obama established many precedents during his presidential campaign, particularly by using new technologies to attract supporters and fundraising. He also attracted unprecedented crowds to hear him speak—at times in the hundreds of thousands of people.

96. Urban. Obama sought the black inner-city experience as a young man, in his search for his own African-American experience. These experiences helped him gain a broader, more complete perspective of America, perhaps filling in gaps that he missed growing up mostly in Hawaii.

97. **Victorious**. The country, as well as the world, reacted to Obama's election as the first African-American president with an enthusiasm for a political figure not seen in many decades. As an unlikely victor in such an important race, millions of people of all backgrounds, races, and politics felt a certain personal satisfaction by Obama's election. He is living proof of his campaign motto, "Yes We Can."

98. **Youthful.** At age 47, Obama is the fifth youngest president to date. Even if he is not the youngest, his youthful athletic appearance, beautiful wife, and two young daughters give him a youthful image, especially as president, a job typically associated with someone much more advanced in age.

99. **Wise**. Throughout his life, people have always listened to his opinions and advice. He is knowledgeable about many things and speaks in ways that are understandable and practical. Obama addresses sensitive and complex issues in a constructive manner, listening to others' viewpoints and opinions to ensure understanding before weighing in on issues.

100. **Winning**. Obama has been a winner in nearly every endeavor he has attempted throughout his life. He is one of those people that seem to find a way to be victorious, sometimes using innovative approaches but always playing within the rules. The only time Obama ever actually experienced defeat was in running for an Illinois congressional seat. He unsuccessfully ran for a seat in the U.S. House of Representatives in 2000, an experience

from which he learned much about what he needed to do to be a winner in the future.

101. **Zestful.** Obama demonstrates a zest in life in everything he does. He created an excitement around him that energized others to support him and his campaign. This zest can be seen, heard, and felt every time you see him and hear him speak.

About the Author

Peter R. Garber is the accomplished author of over 40 books and articles on a variety of workplace topics including training, customer service, supervisory development, human resources, leadership and management. He has worked as a Human Resources Professional for over 25 years in a variety of roles and positions, and is considered an expert in this field.

He lives in Wexford, Pennsylvania, U.S.A.

Did you like this book?

If you enjoyed this book, you will find more interesting books
at

www.MMPubs.com

Please take the time to let us know how you liked this book.
Even short reviews of 2-3 sentences can be helpful and may
be used in our marketing materials. If you take the time to
post a review for this book on Amazon.com, let us know when
the review is posted and you will receive a free audiobook or
ebook from our catalog. Simply email the link to the review
once it is live on Amazon.com, your name, and your mailing
address -- send the email to orders@mmpubs.com with
the subject line "Book Review Posted on Amazon."

If you have questions about this book, our customer
loyalty program, or our review rewards program, please
contact us at info@mmpubs.com.

Multi-Media
Publications Inc.

Your Business Publisher since 1988.

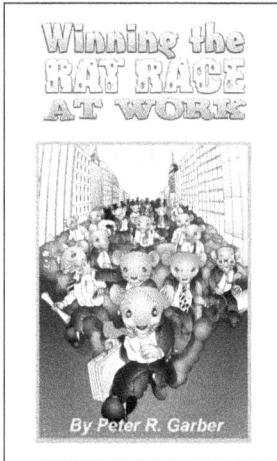

Want to Get Ahead in Your Career?

Do you find yourself challenged by office politics, bad things happen-ing to good careers, dealing with the "big cheeses" at work, the need for effective networking skills, and keeping good working relation-ships with coworkers and bosses?

Winning the Rat Race at Work is a unique book that provides you with case studies, interactive exercises, self-assessments, strategies, evaluations, and models for overcoming these workplace challenges. The book illustrates the stages of a career and the career choices that determine your future, empowering you to make positive changes.

Written by Peter R. Garber, the author of *100 Ways to Get on the Wrong Side of Your Boss*, this book is a must read for anyone interested in getting ahead in his or her career. You will want to keep a copy in your top desk drawer for ready reference whenever you find yourself in a challenging predicament at work.

ISBN: 1-895186-68-4   (paperback)

Also available in ebook formats. Order from your local bookseller, Amazon.com, or directly from the publisher at **www.mmpubs.com/rats**

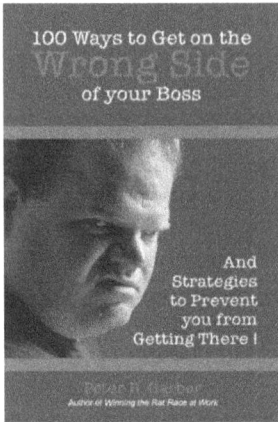

100 Ways to Get on the Wrong Side of your Boss

And Strategies to Prevent you from Getting There !

Peter R. Garber
Author of Winning the Rat Race at Work

Need More Help with the Politics at Work?

100 Ways To Get On The Wrong Side Of Your Boss (And Strategies to Prevent You from Getting There!) was written for anyone who has ever been frustrated by his or her working relationship with the boss—and who hasn't ever felt this way!

Bosses play a critically important role in your career success and getting on the wrong side of this important individual in your working life is not a good thing. Each of these 100 Ways is designed to illustrate a particular problem that you may encounter when dealing with your boss and then an effective strategy to prevent this problem from reoccurring. You will learn how to deal more effectively with your boss in this fun and practical book filled with invaluable advice that can be utilized every day at work.

Written by Peter R. Garber, the author of *Winning the Rat Race at Work*, this book is a must read for anyone inter-ested in getting ahead. You will want to keep a copy in your top desk drawer for ready reference whenever you find yourself in a challenging predicament at work.

ISBN: 1-895186-98-6   (paperback)

Order from your local bookseller, Amazon.com, or directly from the publisher at   **www.InTroubleAtWork.com**

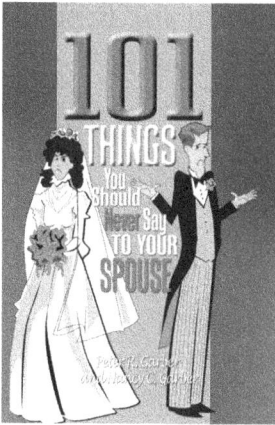

Stay out of the Doghouse

Let's face it – men and women don't speak the same language. We may be using the same words, but what we say and what we mean may be two completely different things. The miscommunications that arise from different interpretations of various comments can lead to major arguments and even break up a marriage.

This book presents some common misunderstood statements and explains both the intended meaning and a range of alternate interpretations. Best of all, the book provides advice on how to avoid these misunderstandings in the first place.

Learn how to get your ideas across more clearly to your spouse in a way that is not as likely to trigger a burst of tears, slammed doors, or the dreaded "cold shoulder" and build a happier marriage..

ISBN: 9781897326008 (paperback)
ISBN: 9781897326015 (Adobe PDF eBook)

Order from your local bookseller, Amazon.com, or directly from the publisher at **www.mmpubs.com**

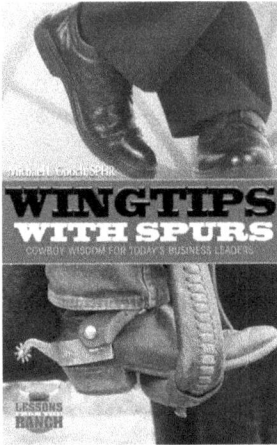

Lessons from the Ranch for Today's Business Manager

The lure of the open plain, boots, chaps and cowboy hats makes us think of a different and better way of life. The cowboy code of honor is an image that is alive and well in our hearts and minds, and its wisdom is timeless.

Using ranch based stories, author Michael Gooch, a ranch owner, tells us how to apply cowboy wisdom to our everyday management challenges. Serving up straight forward, practical advice, the book deals with issues of dealing with conflict, strategic thinking, ethics, having fun at work, hiring and firing, building strong teams, and knowing when to run from trouble.

A unique (and fun!) approach to management training, Wingtips with Spurs is a must read whether you are new to management or a grizzled veteran.

ISBN: 1-897326-88-2   (paperback)

Also available in ebook formats. Order from your local bookseller, Amazon.com, or directly from the publisher at **www.mmpubs.com**

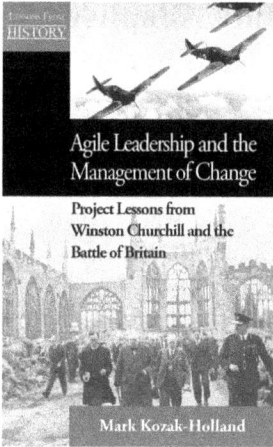

Agile Leadership and the Management of Change: Project Lessons from Winston Churchill and the Battle of Britain

Around the turn of the millennium, there was a poll that asked who was the most influential person in all of Britain's history. The winner: Winston Churchill. What distinguished him were his leadership qualities: his ability to create and share a powerful vision, his ability to motivate the population in the face of tremendous fear, and his ability to get others to rally behind him and quickly turn his visions into reality. By any measure, Winston Churchill was a powerful leader.

What many don't know, however, was how Churchill used his leadership skills to restructure the British military, government, and even the British manufacturing sector to get ready for an imminent enemy invasion in early 1940.

Learn how Churchill led a massive change project that affected the daily lives of millions of people, and learn how they can be applied to today's projects.

ISBN: 9781554890354 (paperback)
ISBN: 9781554890361 (PDF ebook)

http://www.mmpubs.com/

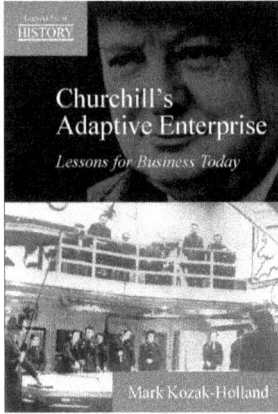

Churchill's Adaptive Enterprise: Lessons for Business Today

This book analyzes a period of time from World War II when Winston Churchill, one of history's most famous leaders, faced near defeat for the British in the face of sustained German attacks. The book describes the strategies he used to overcome incredible odds and turn the tide on the impending invasion. The historical analysis is done through a modern business and information technology lens, describing Churchill's actions and strategy using modern business tools and techniques.

Aimed at business executives, IT managers, and project managers, the book extracts learnings from Churchill's experiences that can be applied to business problems today. Particular themes in the book are knowledge management, information portals, adaptive enterprises, and organizational agility.

ISBN: 1-895186-19-6   (paperback)
ISBN: 1-895186-20-X   (PDF ebook)

http://www.mmpubs.com/churchill

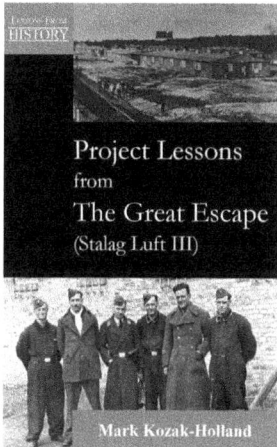

Project Lessons from The Great Escape (Stalag Luft III)

While you might think your project plan is perfect, would you bet your life on it?

In World War II, a group of 220 captured airmen did just that – they staked the lives of everyone in the camp on the success of a project to secretly build a series of tunnels out of a prison camp their captors thought was escape proof.

The prisoners formally structured their work as a project, using the project organization techniques of the day. This book analyzes their efforts using modern project management methods and the nine knowledge areas of the *Guide to the Project Management Body of Knowledge* (PMBoK).

Learn from the successes and mistakes of a project where people really put their lives on the line.

ISBN: 1-895186-80-3   (paperback)
Also available in ebook formats.

http://www.mmpubs.com/escape

www.ingramcontent.com/pod-product-compliance
Lightning Source LLC
Chambersburg PA
CBHW072201270326
41930CB00011B/2501